MW01697923

Mandala Daydream

- A COLOR JOURNEY INTO YOUR INNER MIND -

BY: Karen Sue Chen

Check out KarenSueStudios.com for free coloring pages!
Share your work! #KarenSueStudios on social media.

Printed in the United States of America

First Printing, 2019

ISBN 978-1-7339947-1-2

www.KarenSueStudios.com

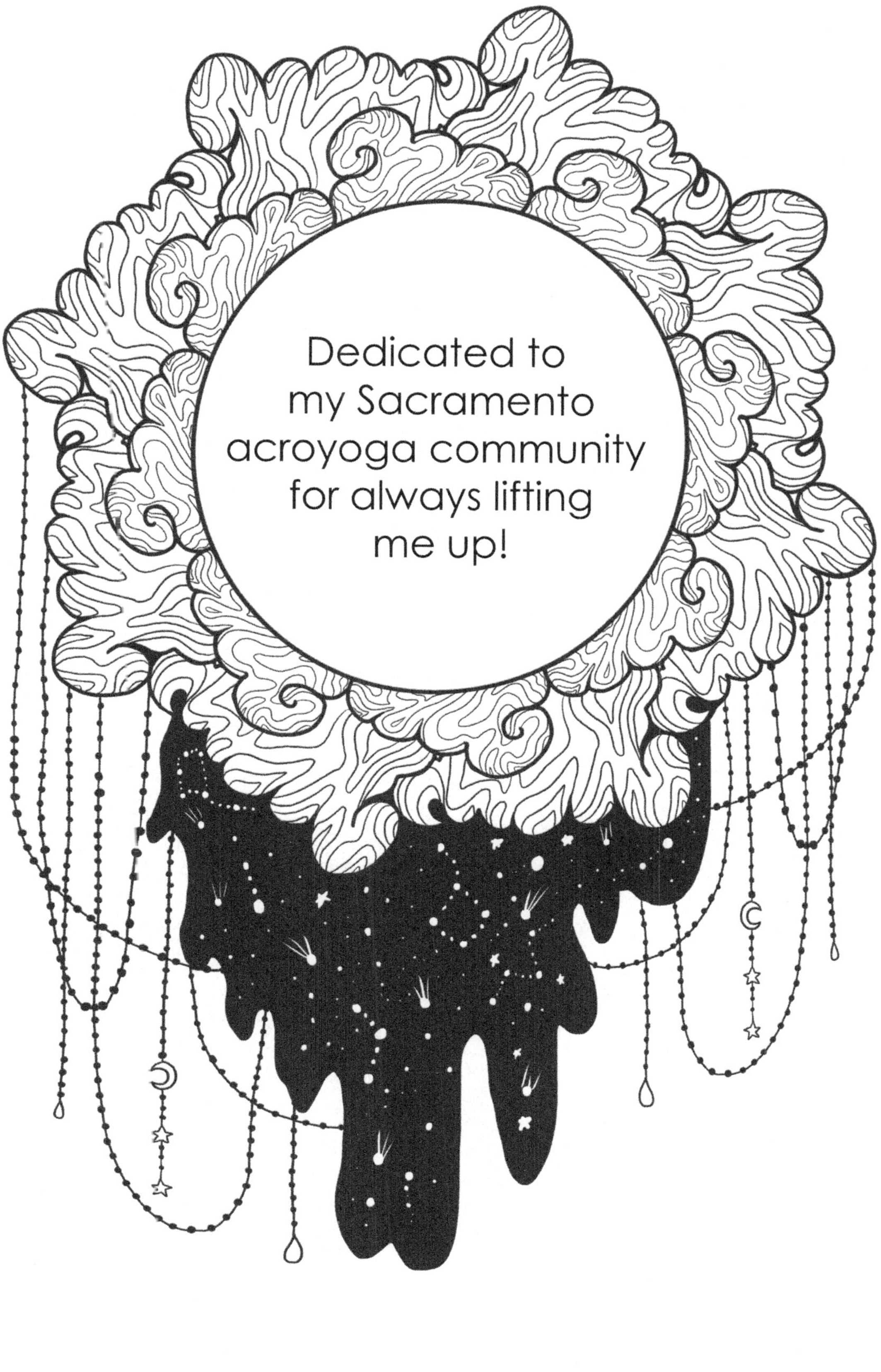
Dedicated to
my Sacramento
acroyoga community
for always lifting
me up!

A Note From the Author:

Thank you so much for purchasing Mandala Daydream! Your support allows me to pursue my dream of being a professional artist. I was born and raised in Texas, and I currently live in California. In my free time I enjoy gardening, yoga, acrobatics, crafting, and hanging out with my pet rabbit Joey.

If you enjoyed this book, check out my other two coloring books, Life of the Wild and Flora and Fauna, on Amazon.

It truly brings me joy to see your finished masterpieces! Please tag @KarenSueStudios or use #karensuestudios.

And always remember to follow your dreams!

Love,

Karen Sue Chen

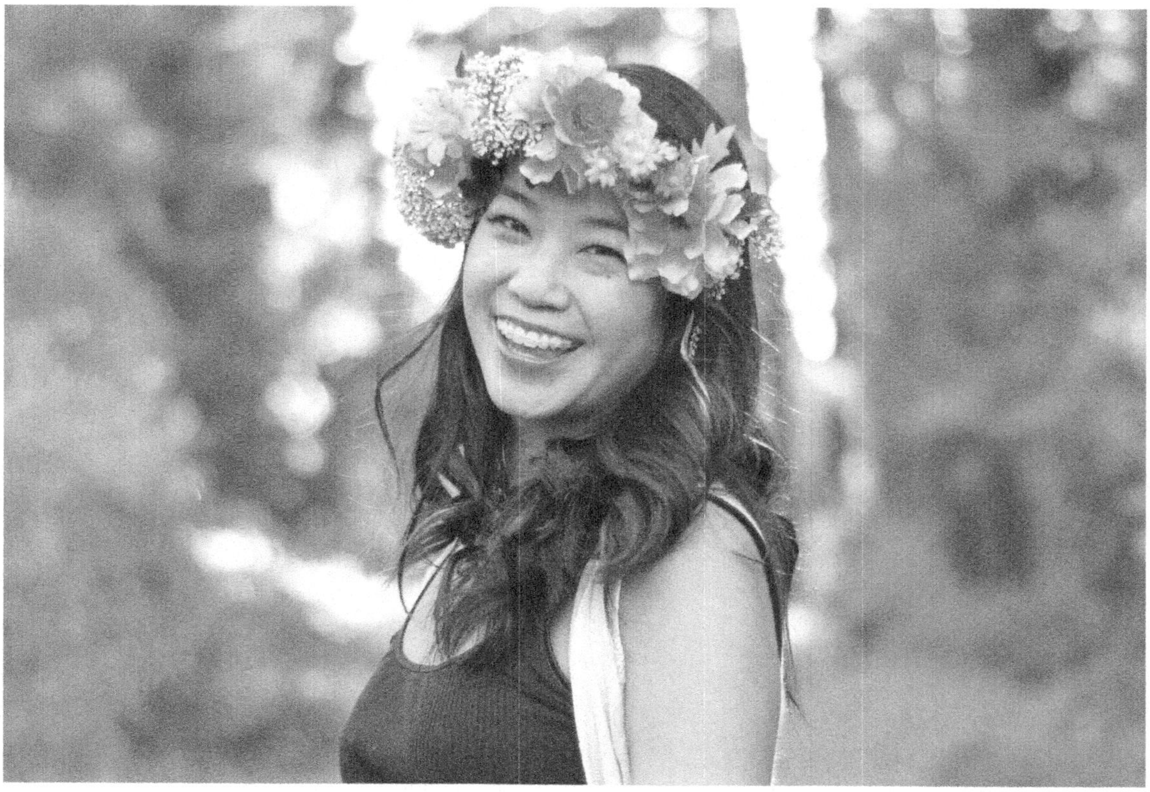

YouTube @KarenSueStudios

Share your work! #KarenSueStudios on social media.

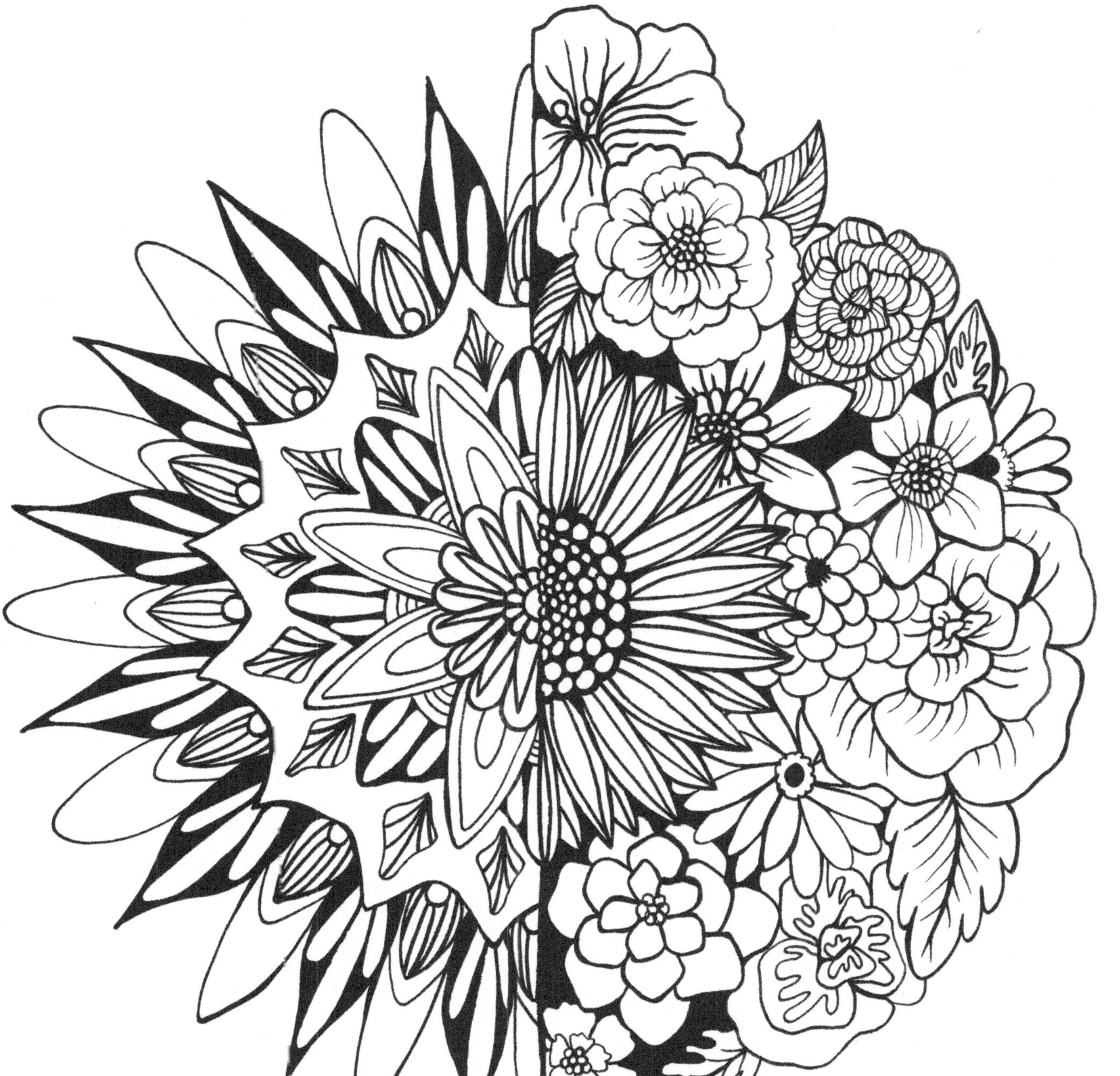

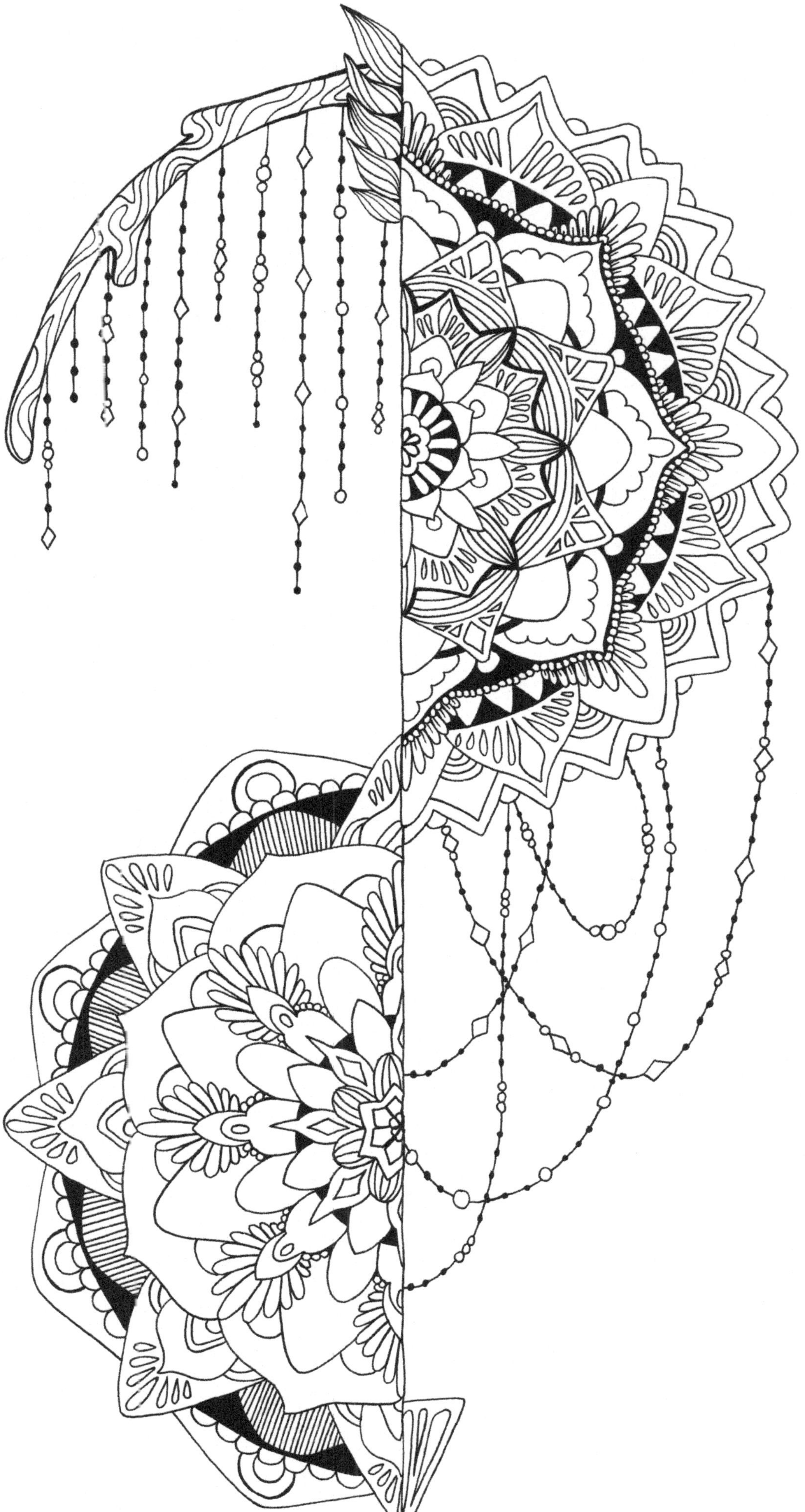

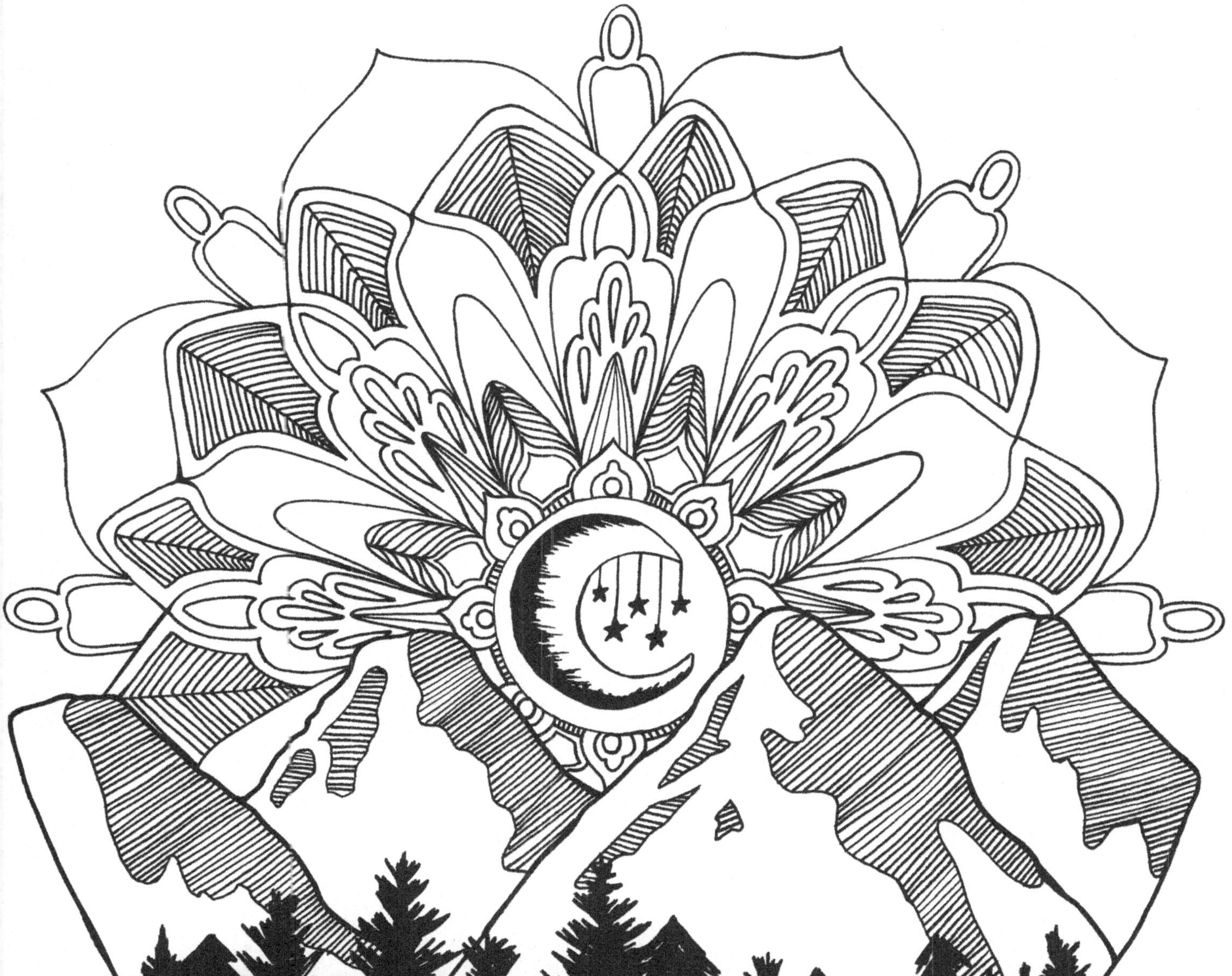

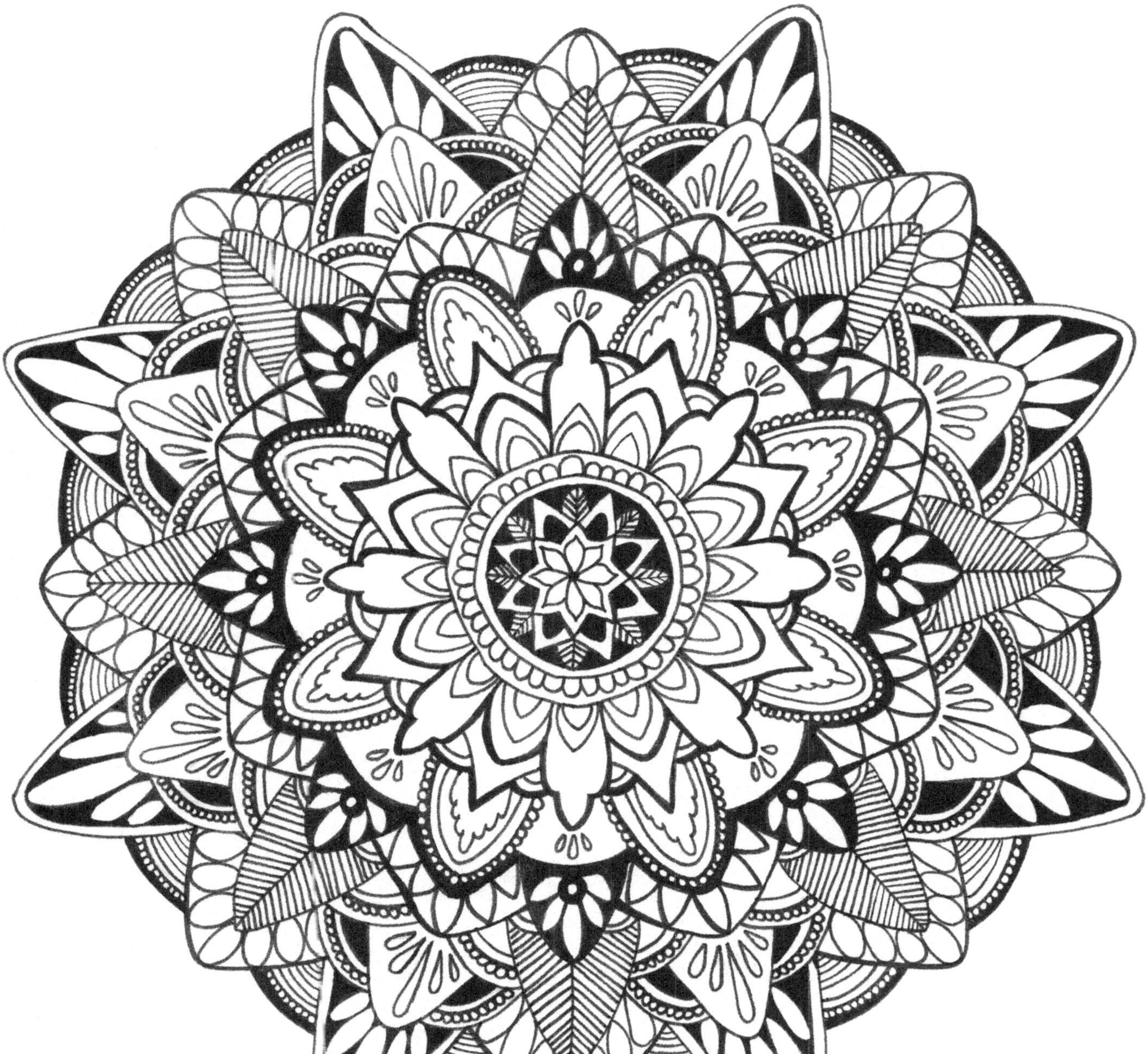

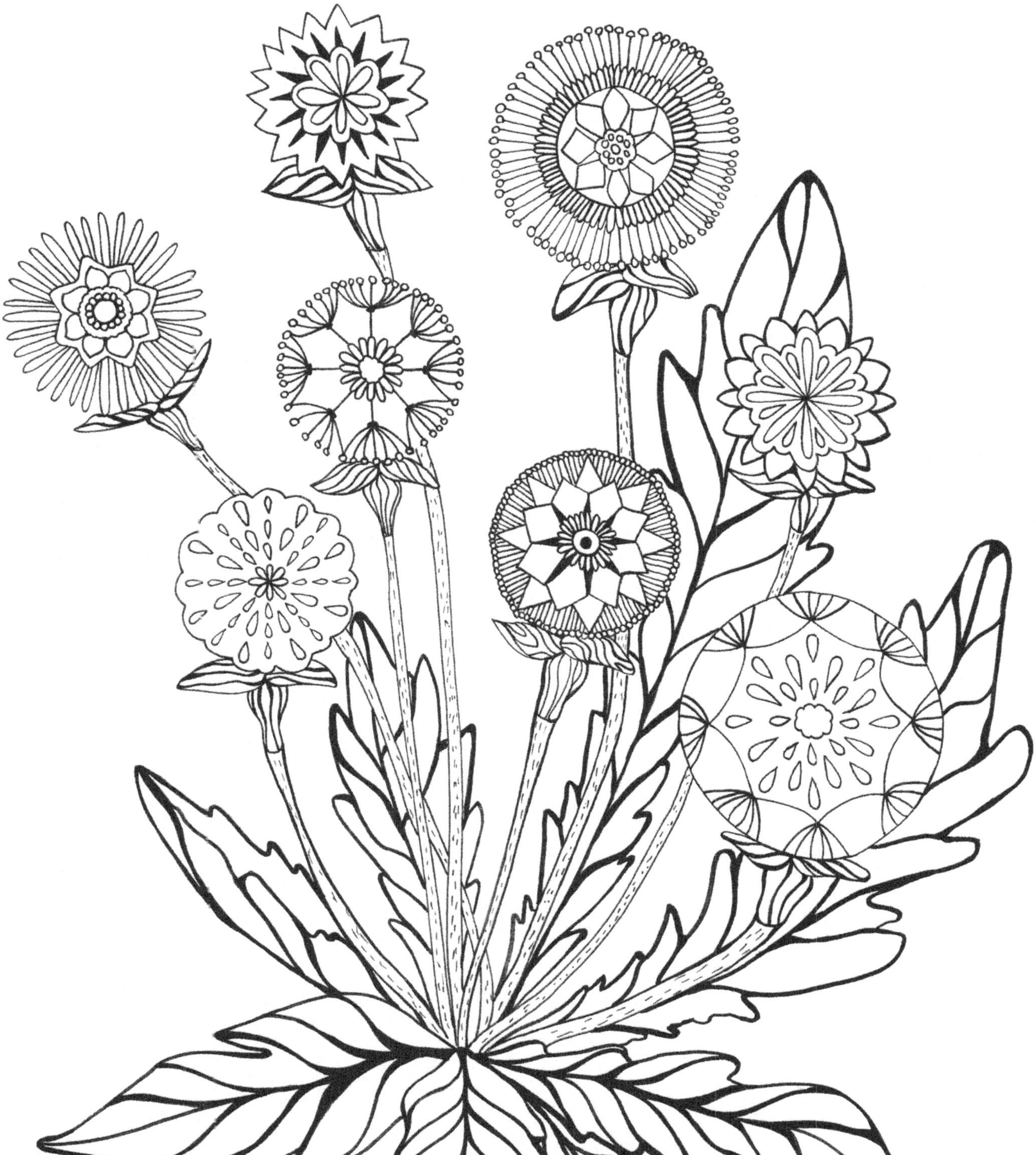

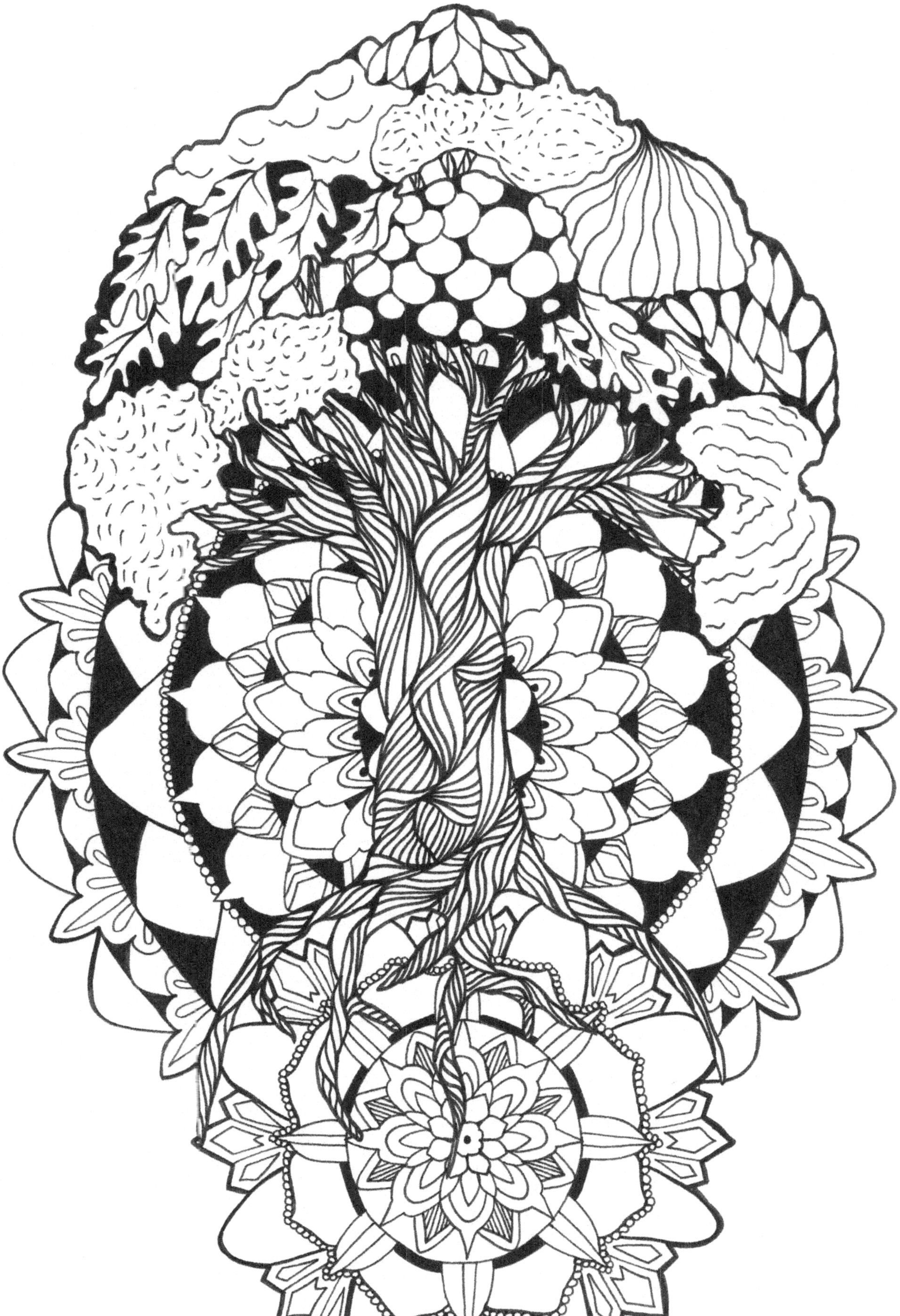

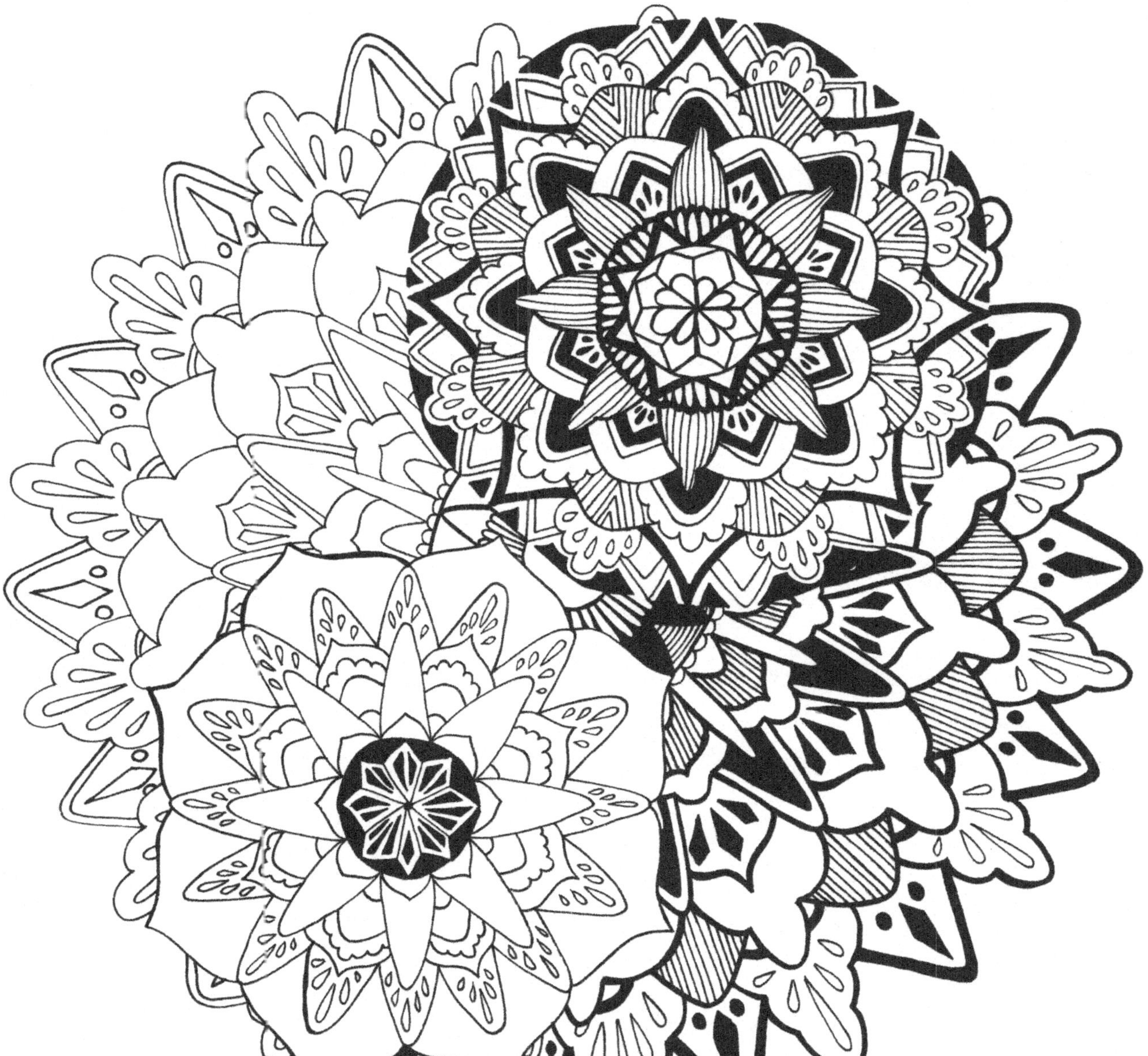

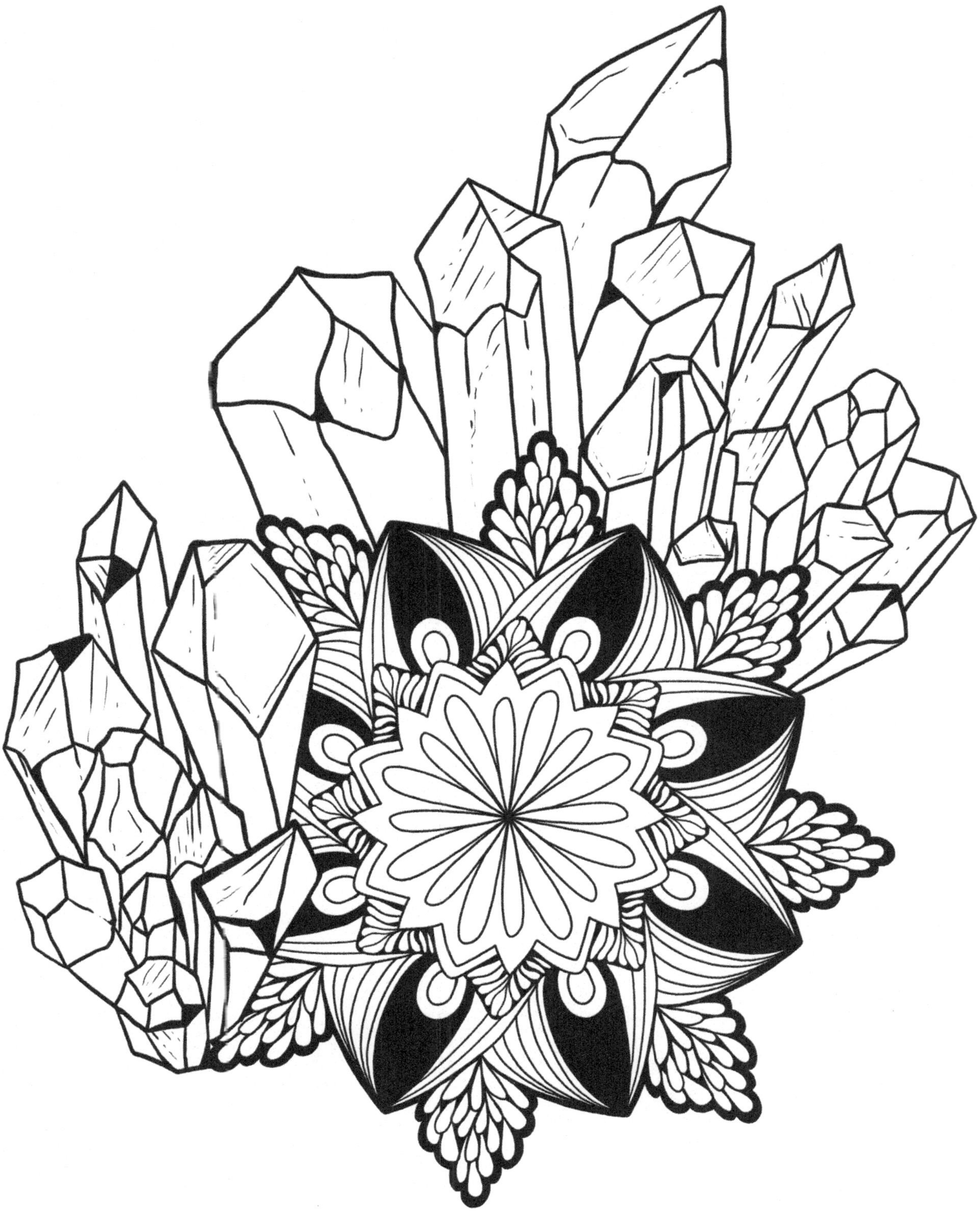

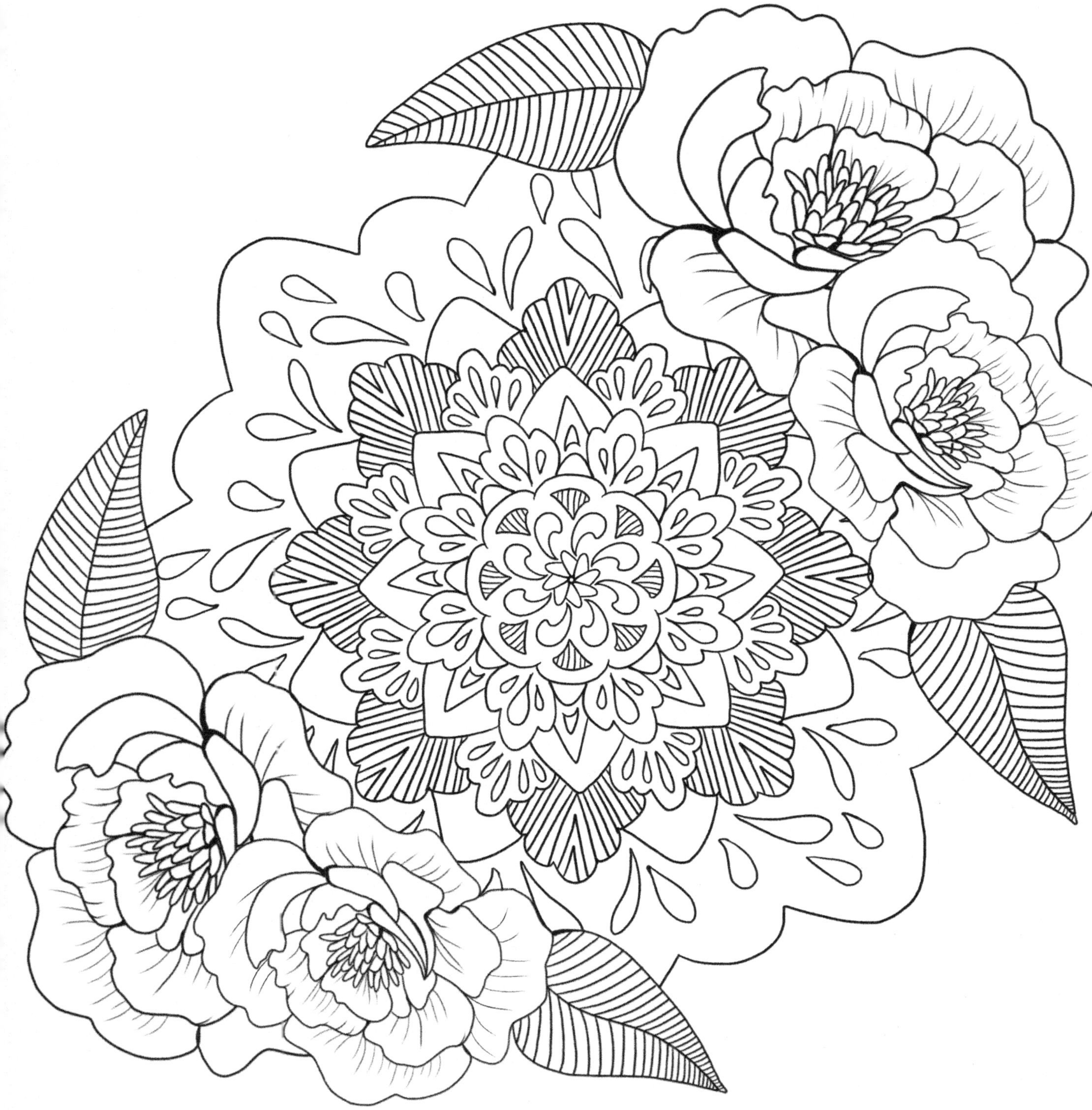

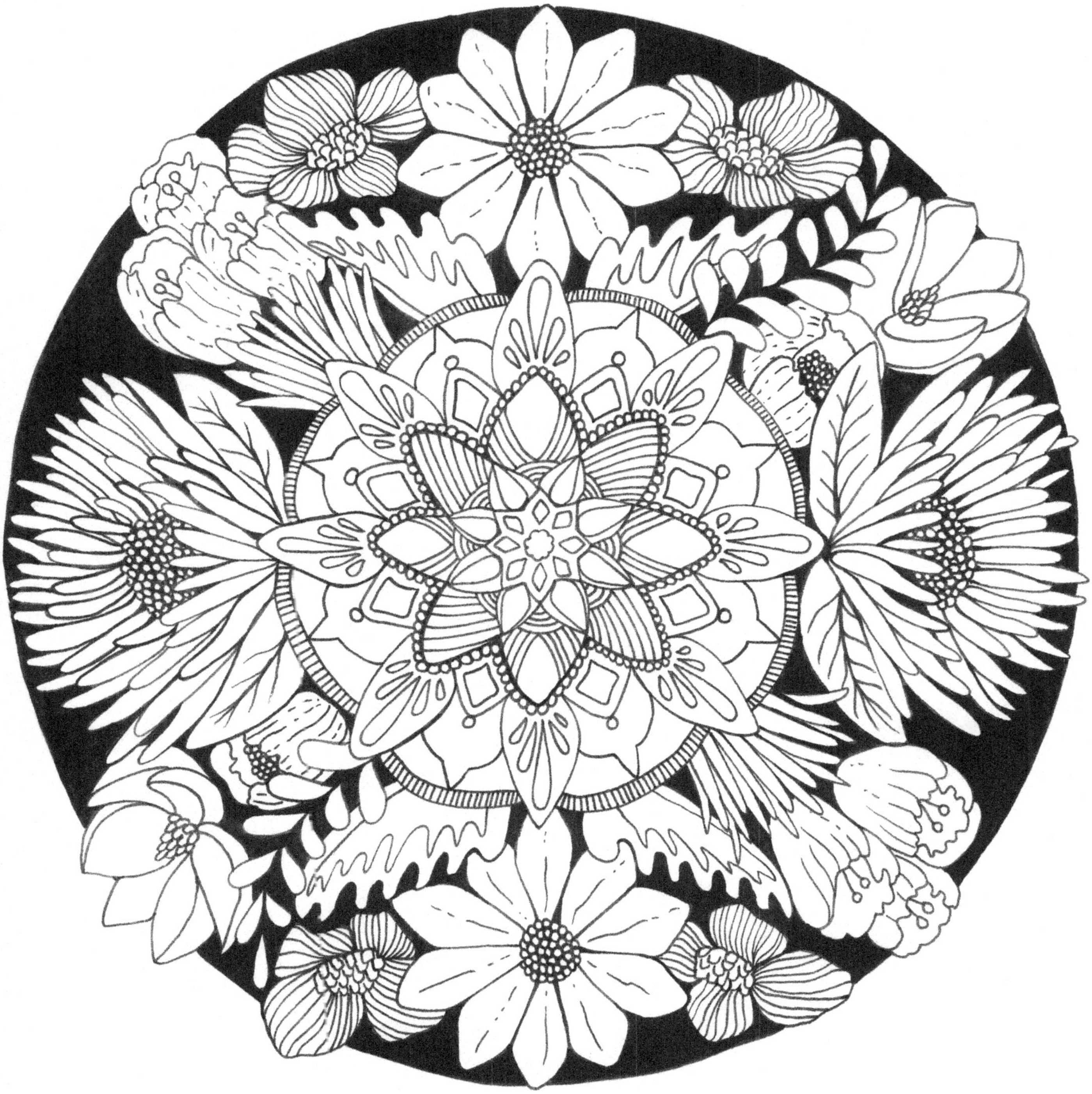

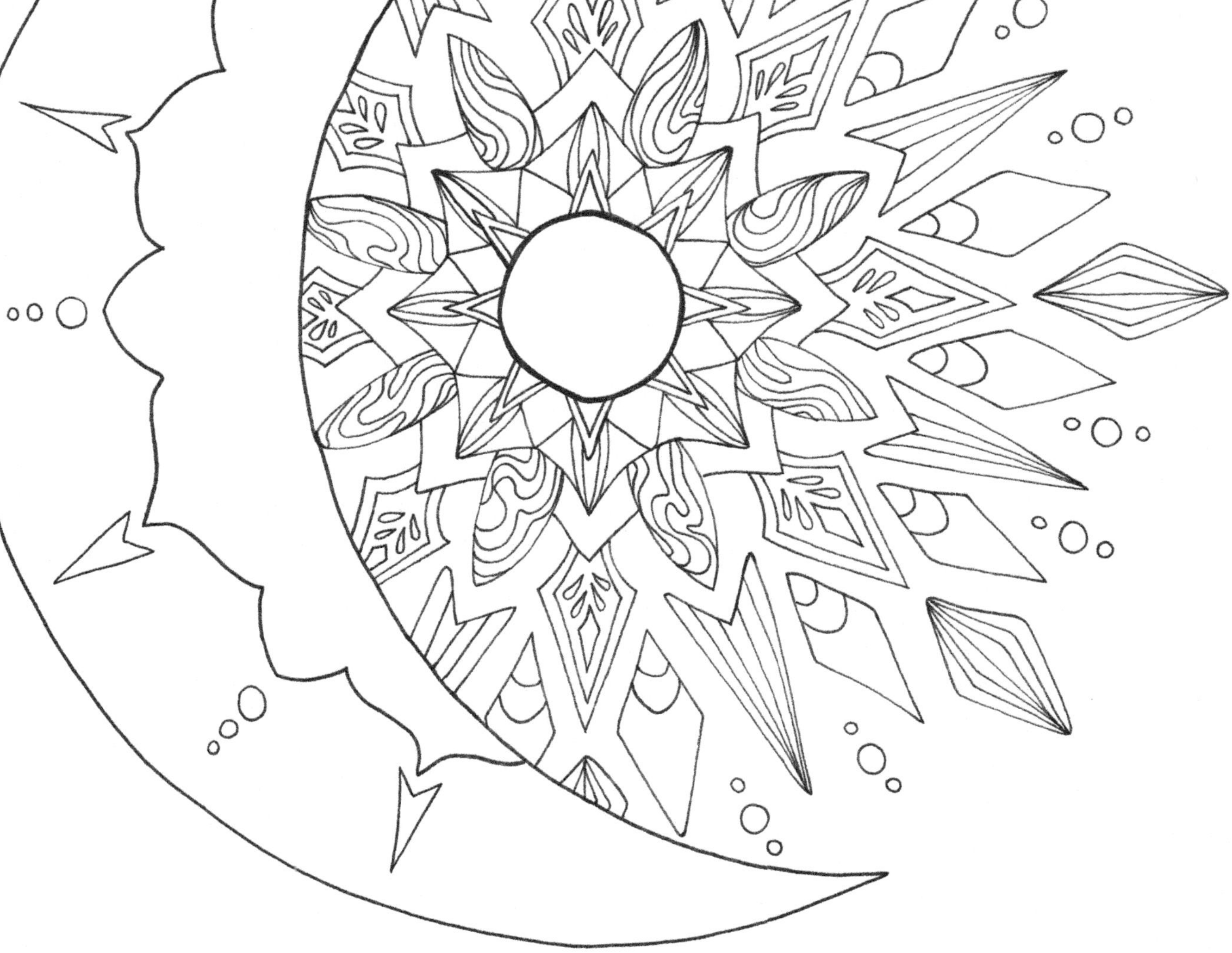

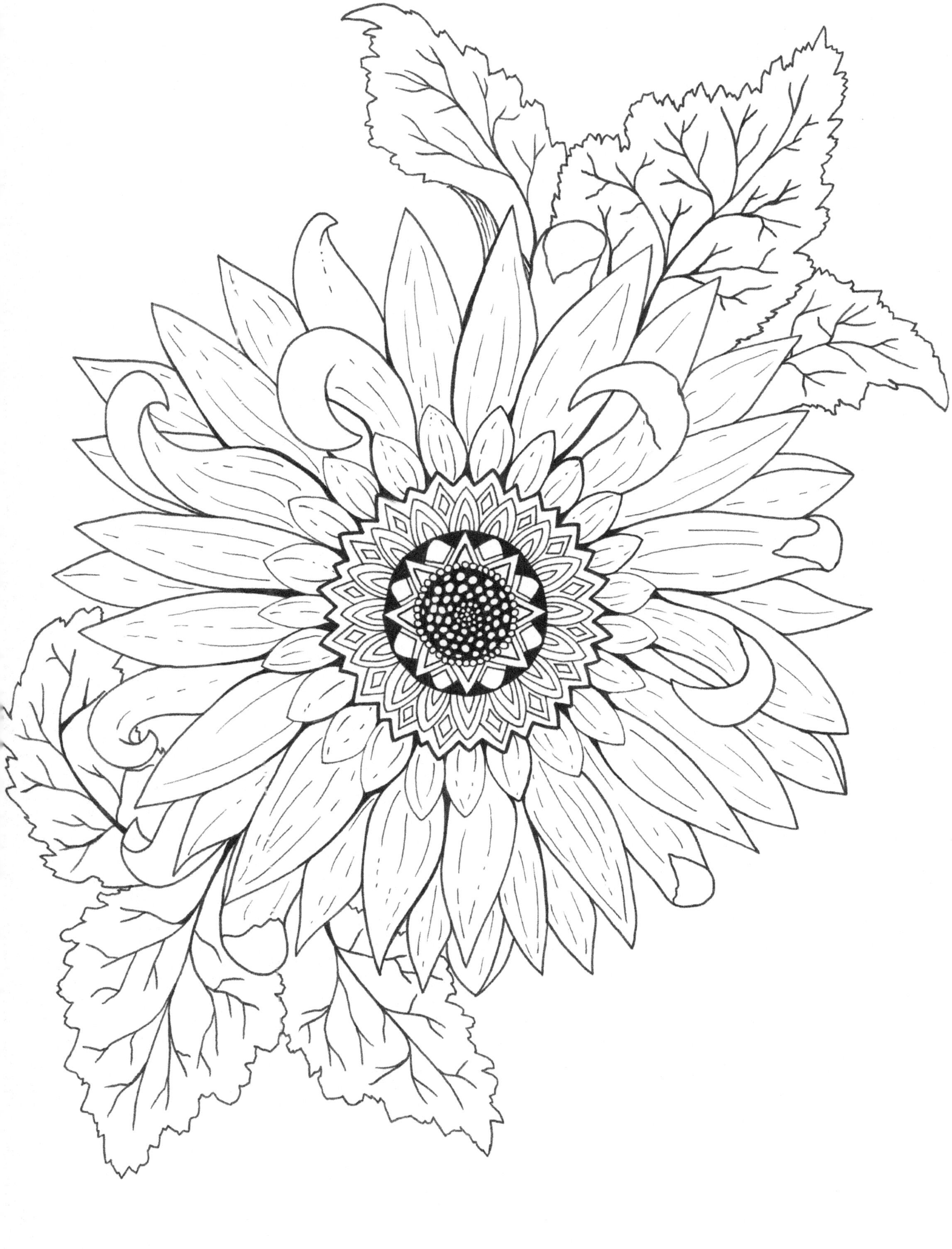

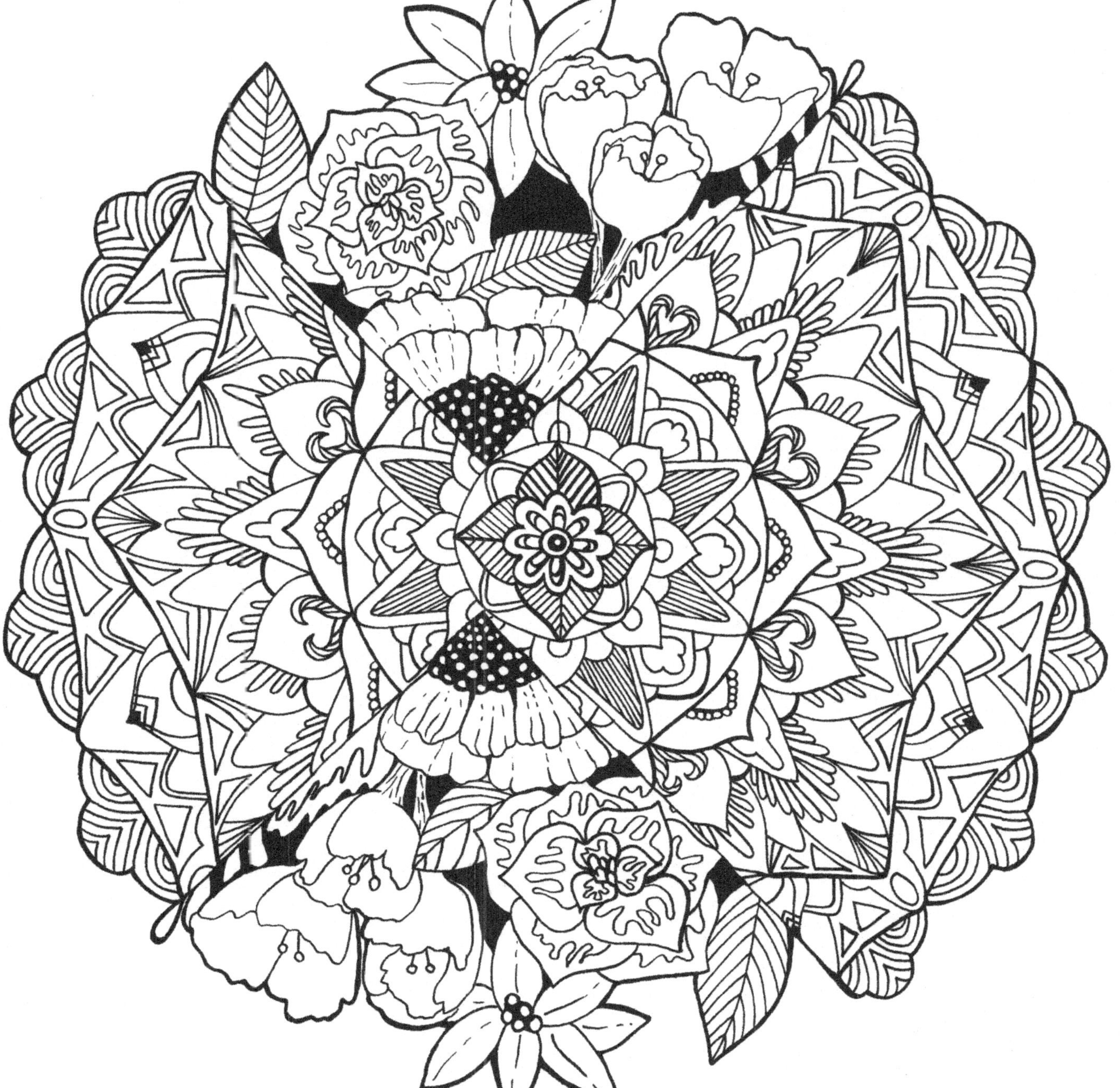

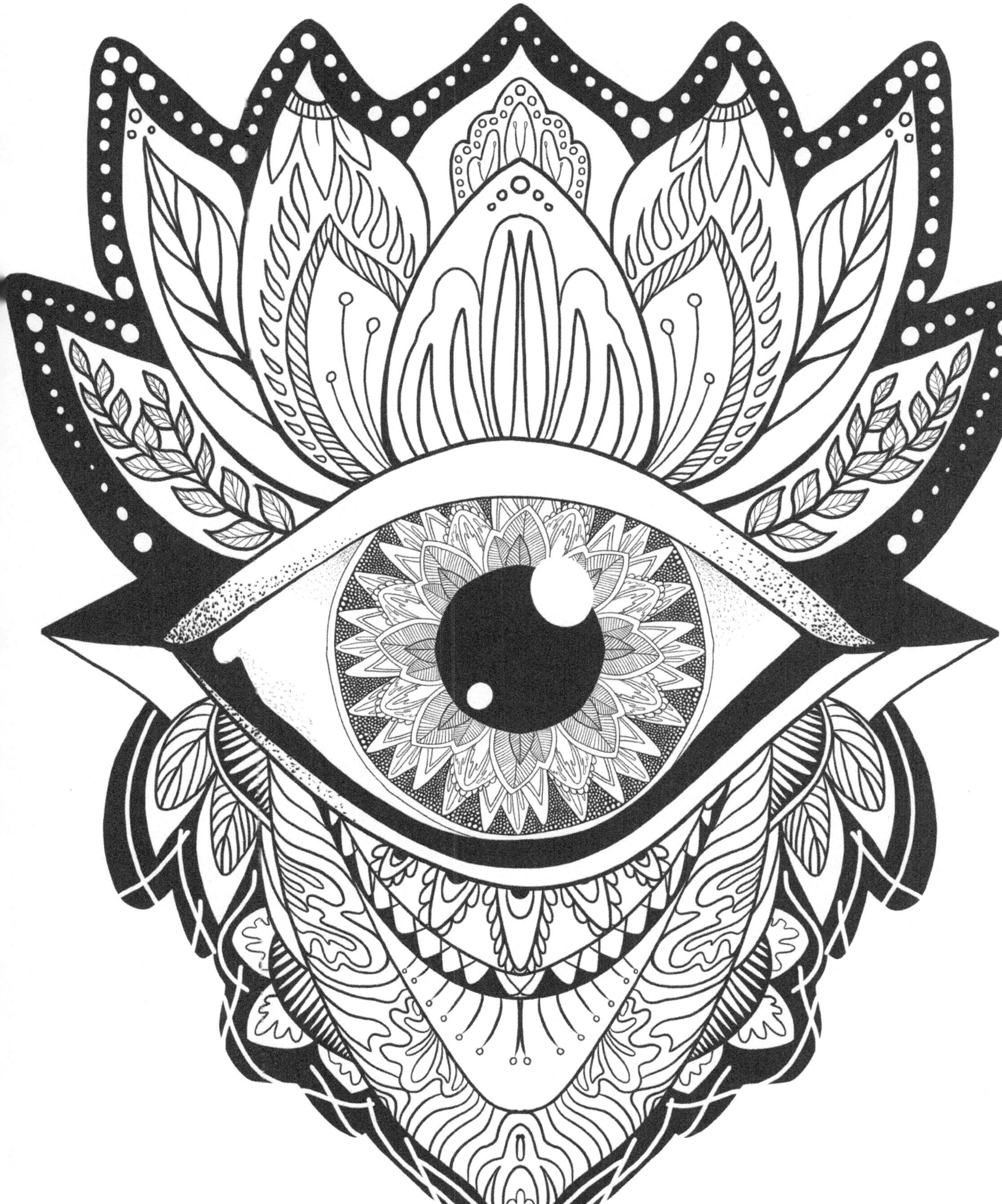

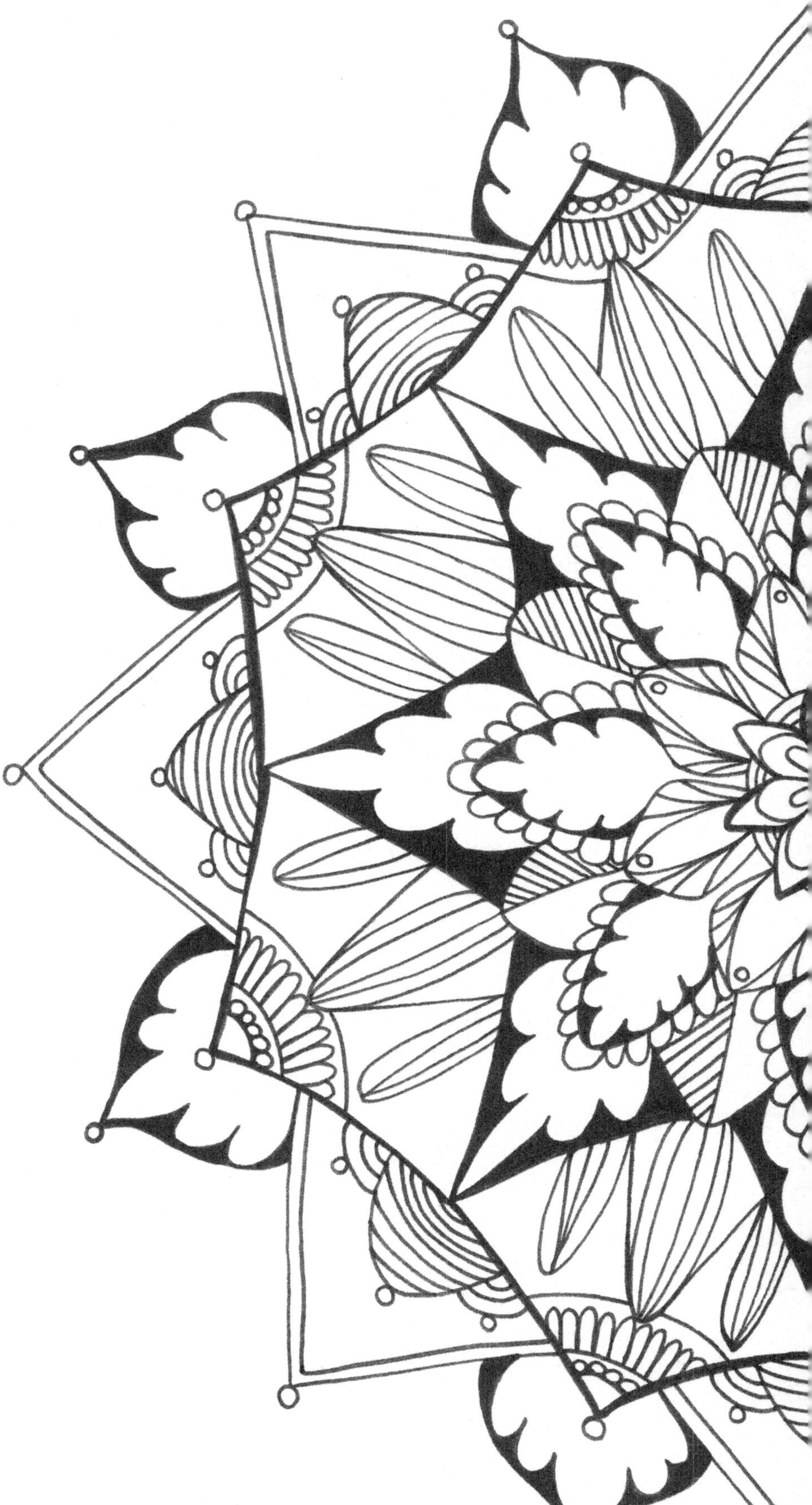

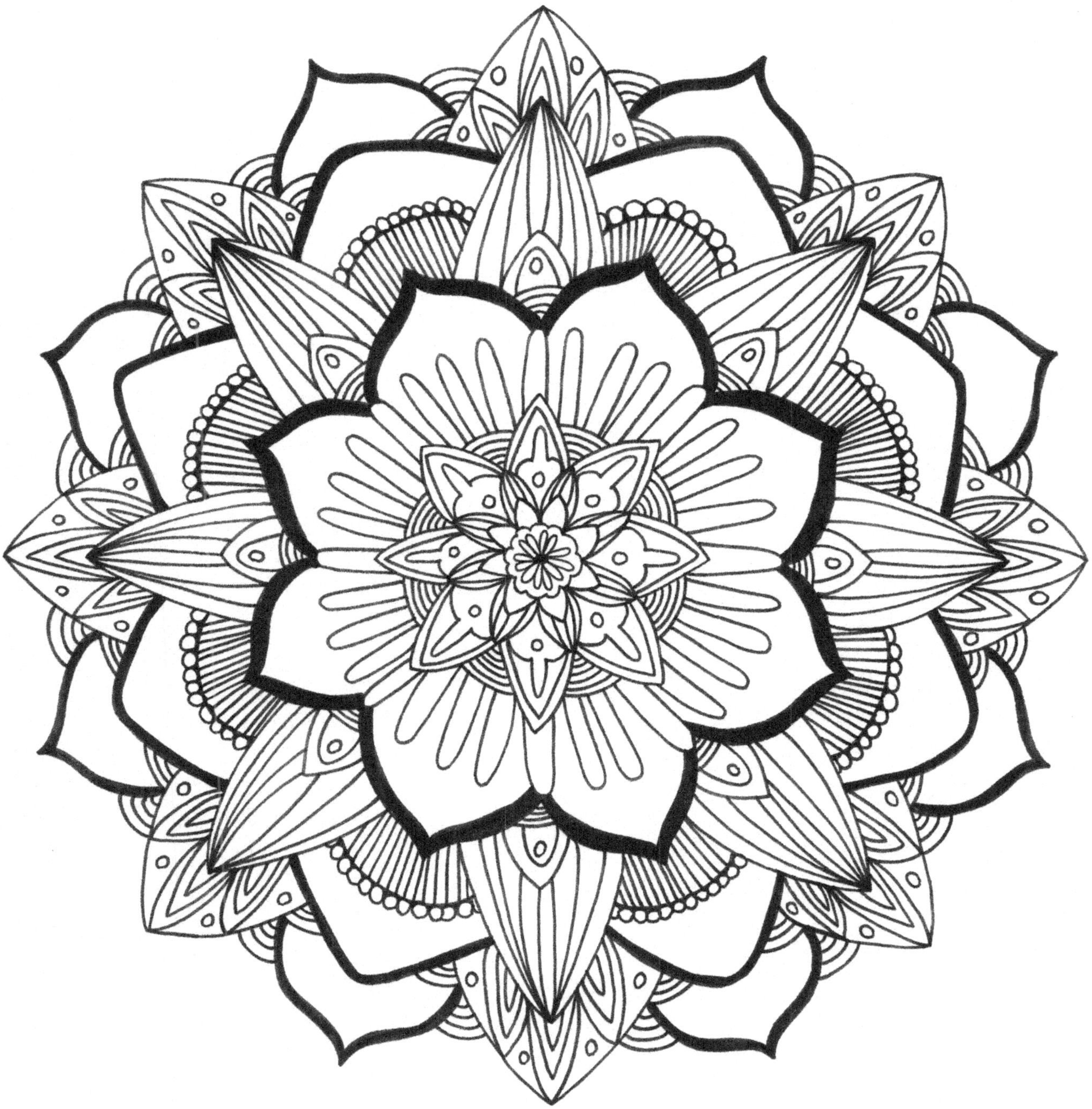

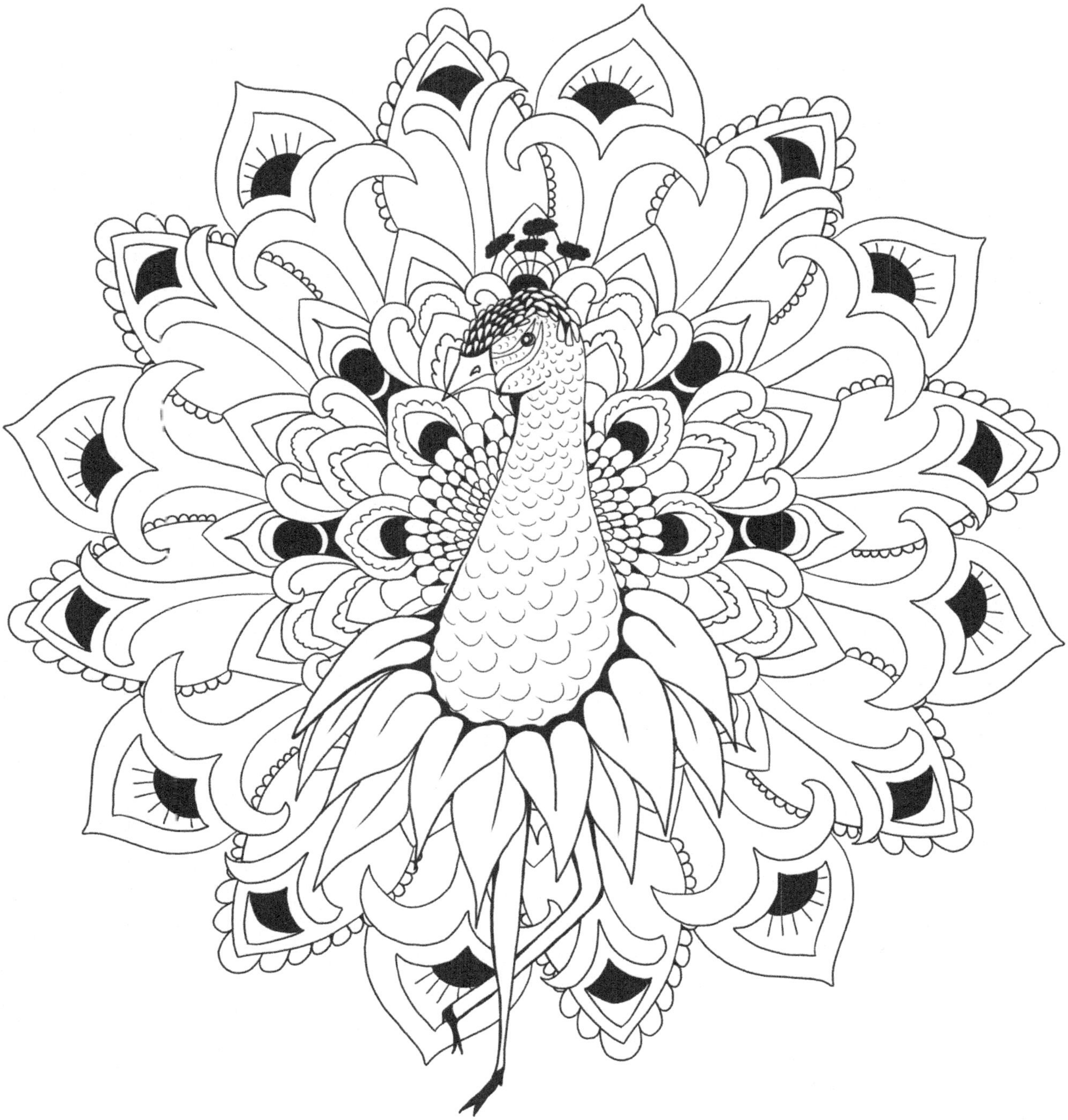

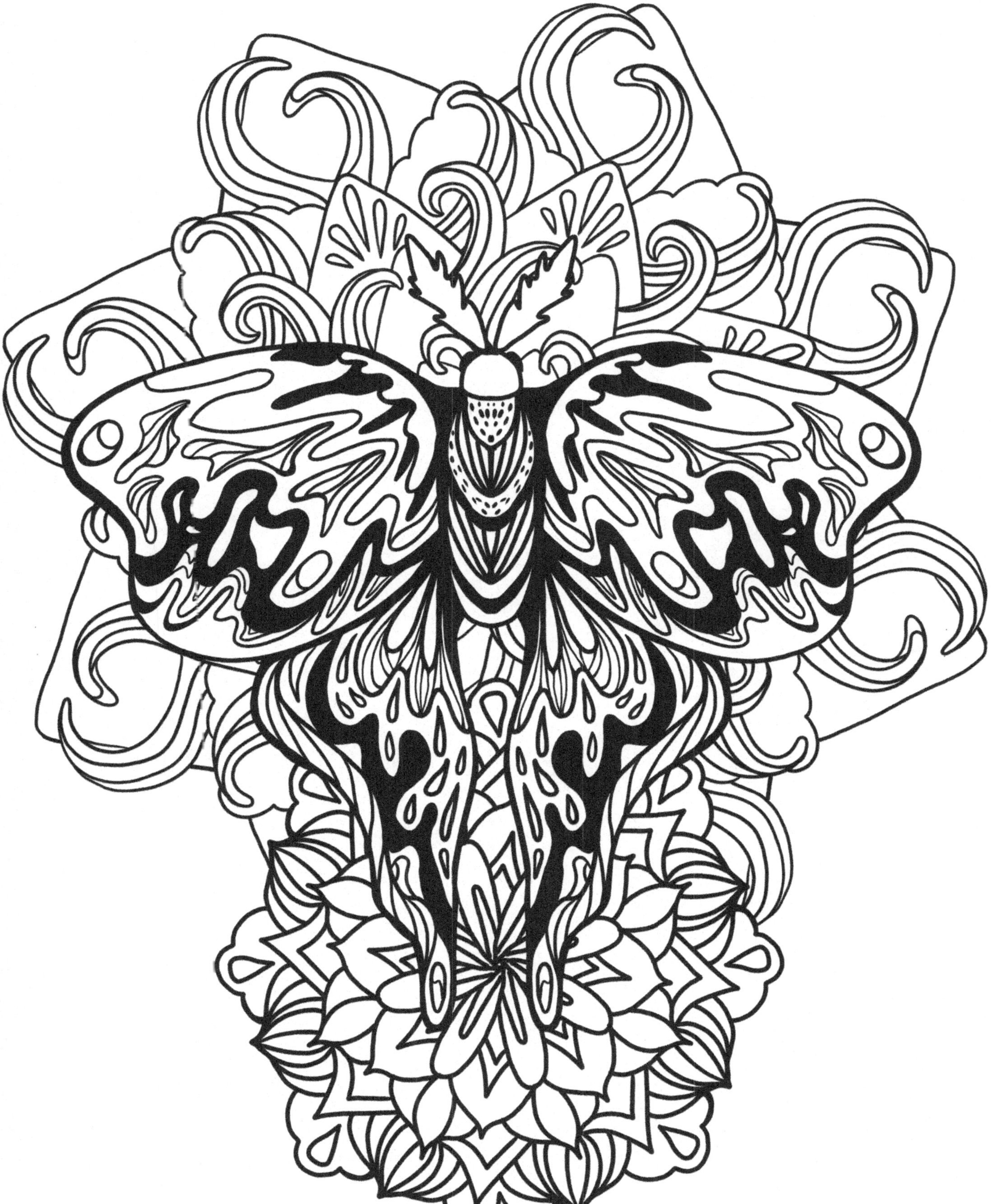

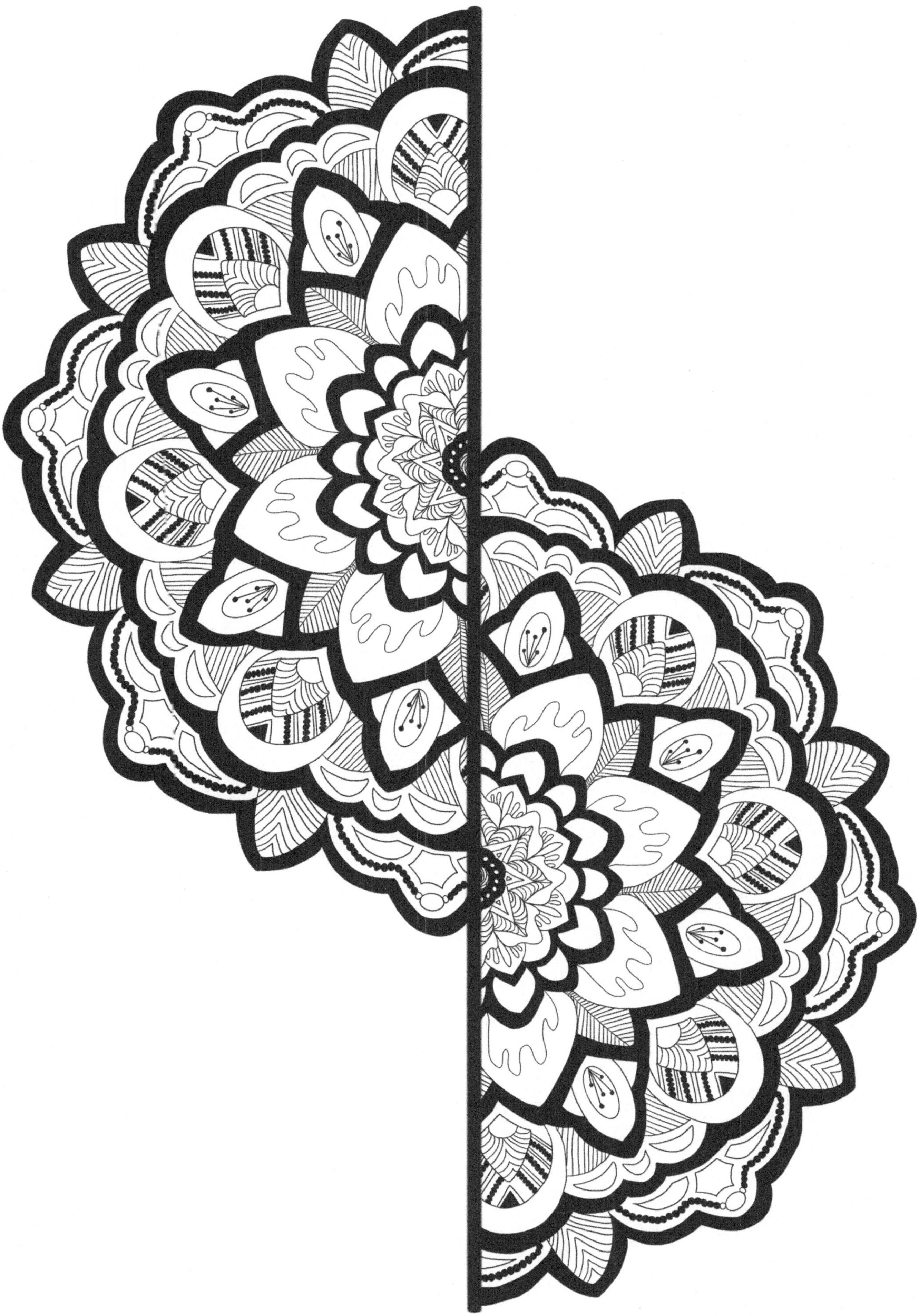

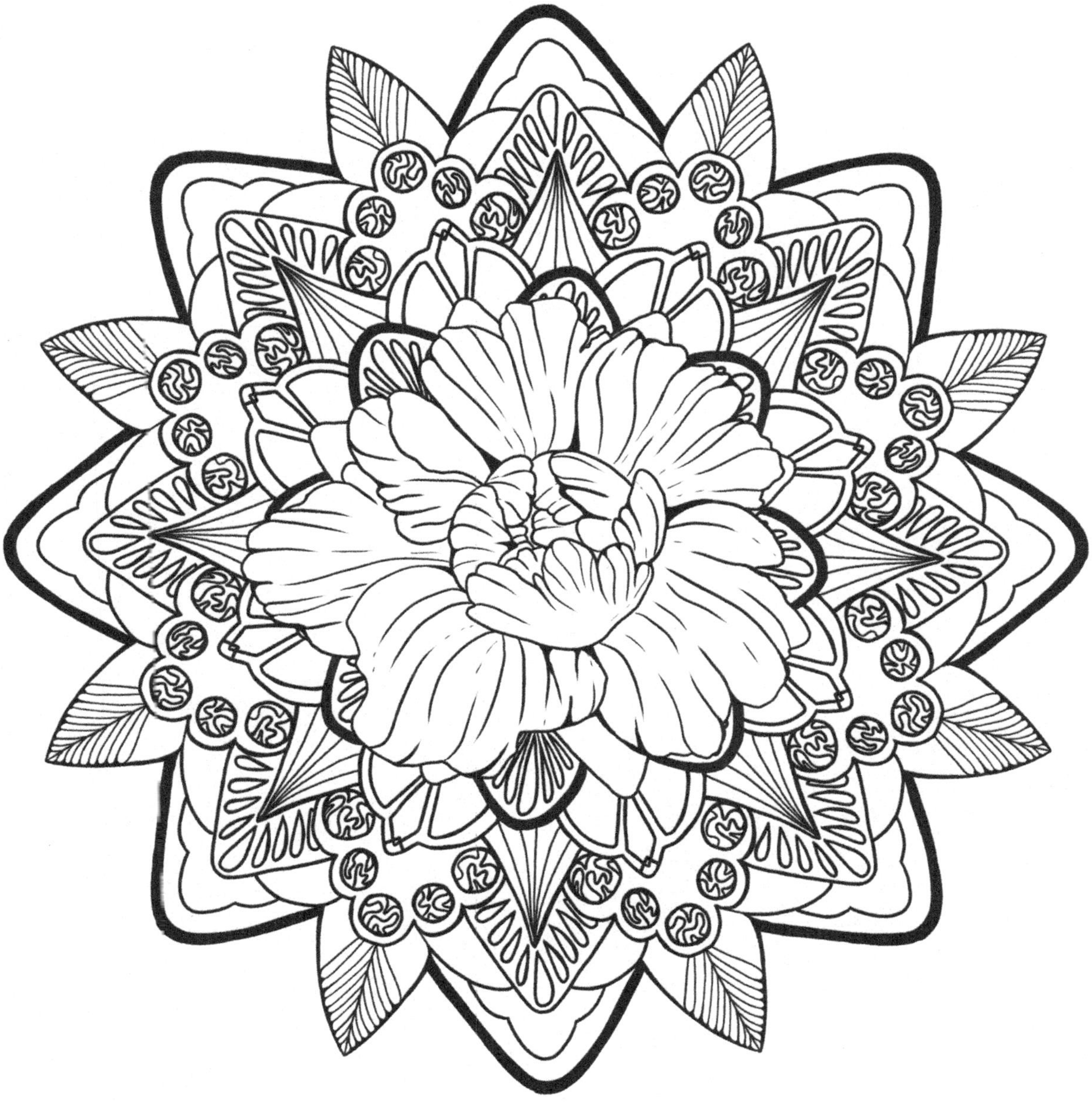

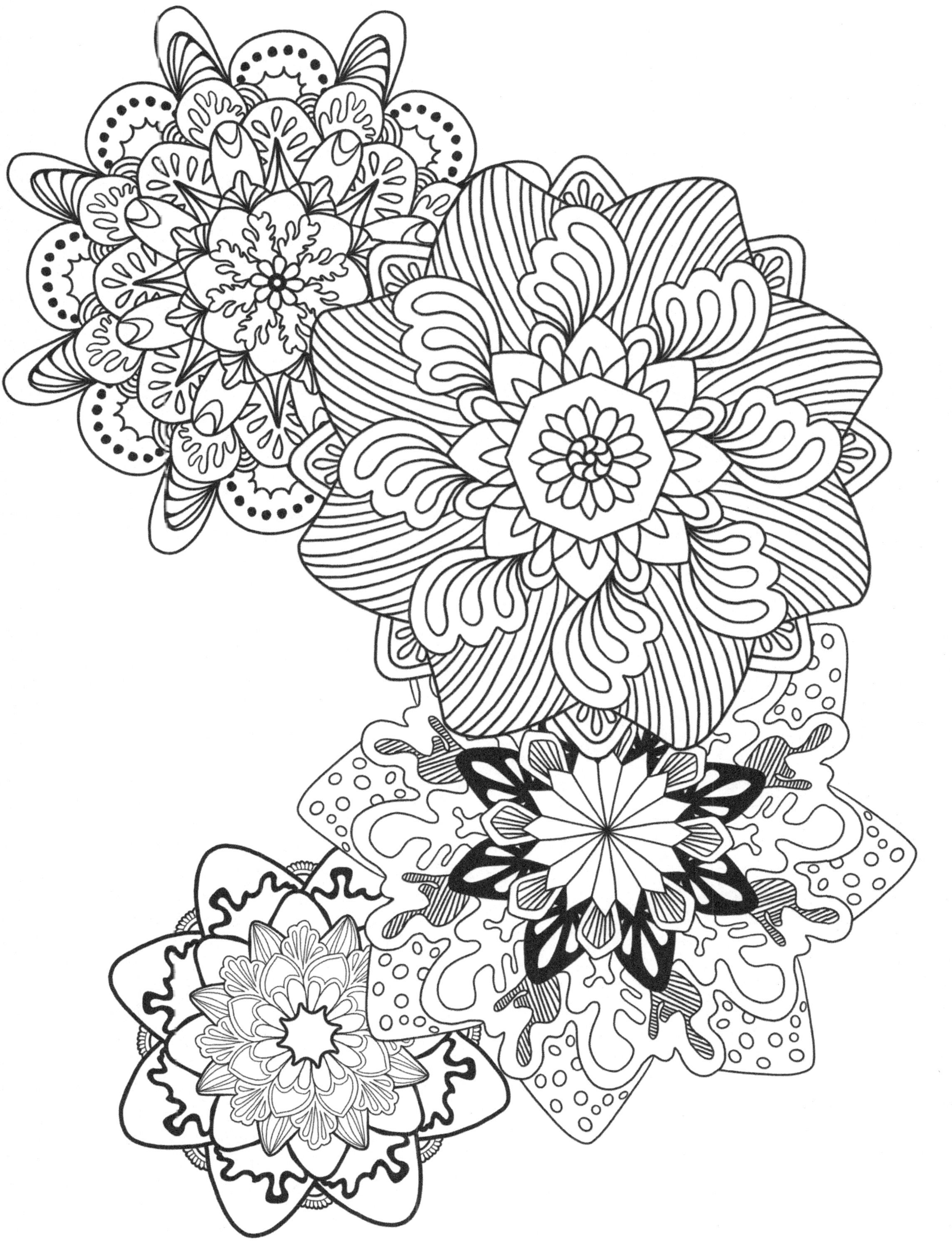

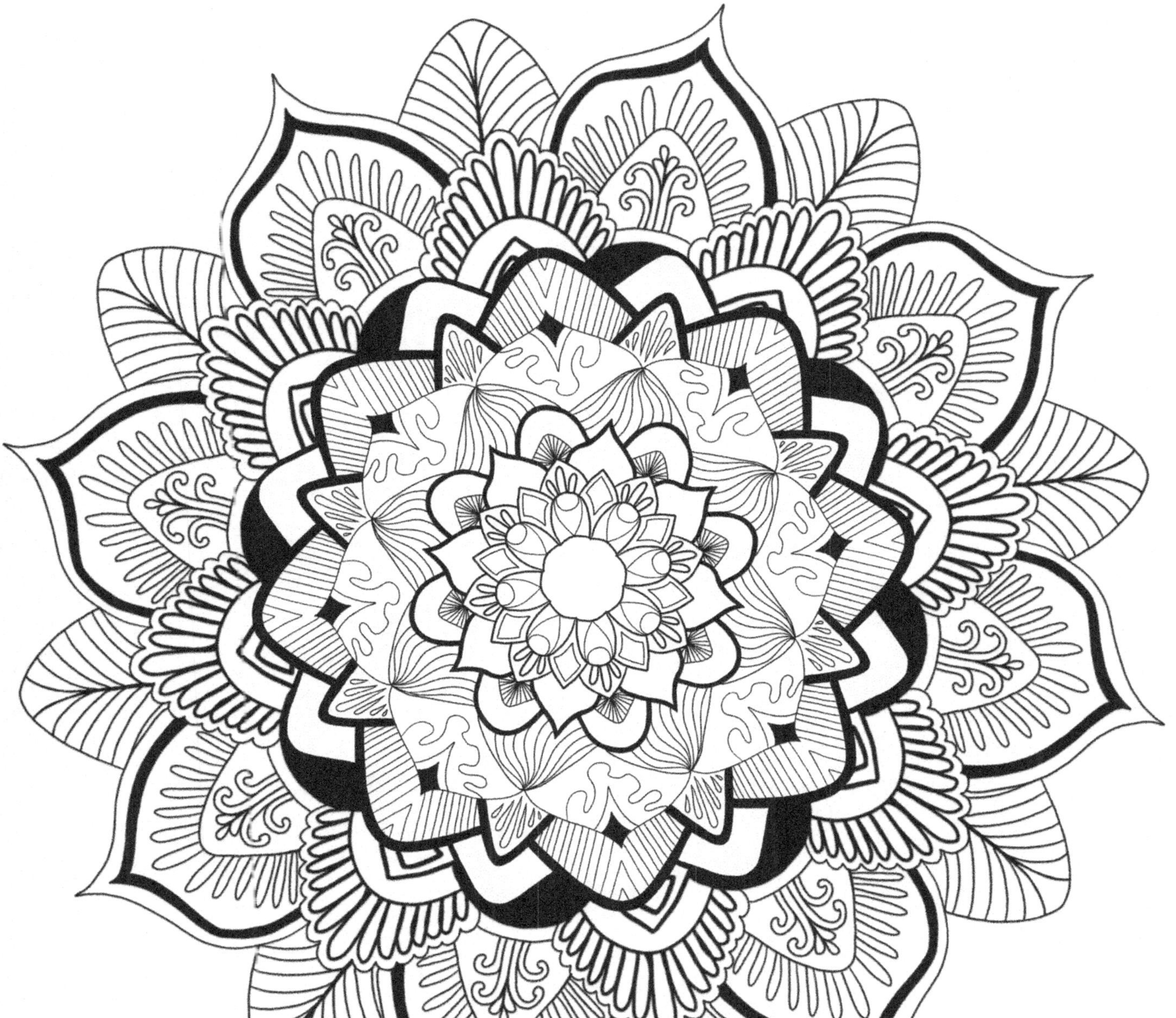

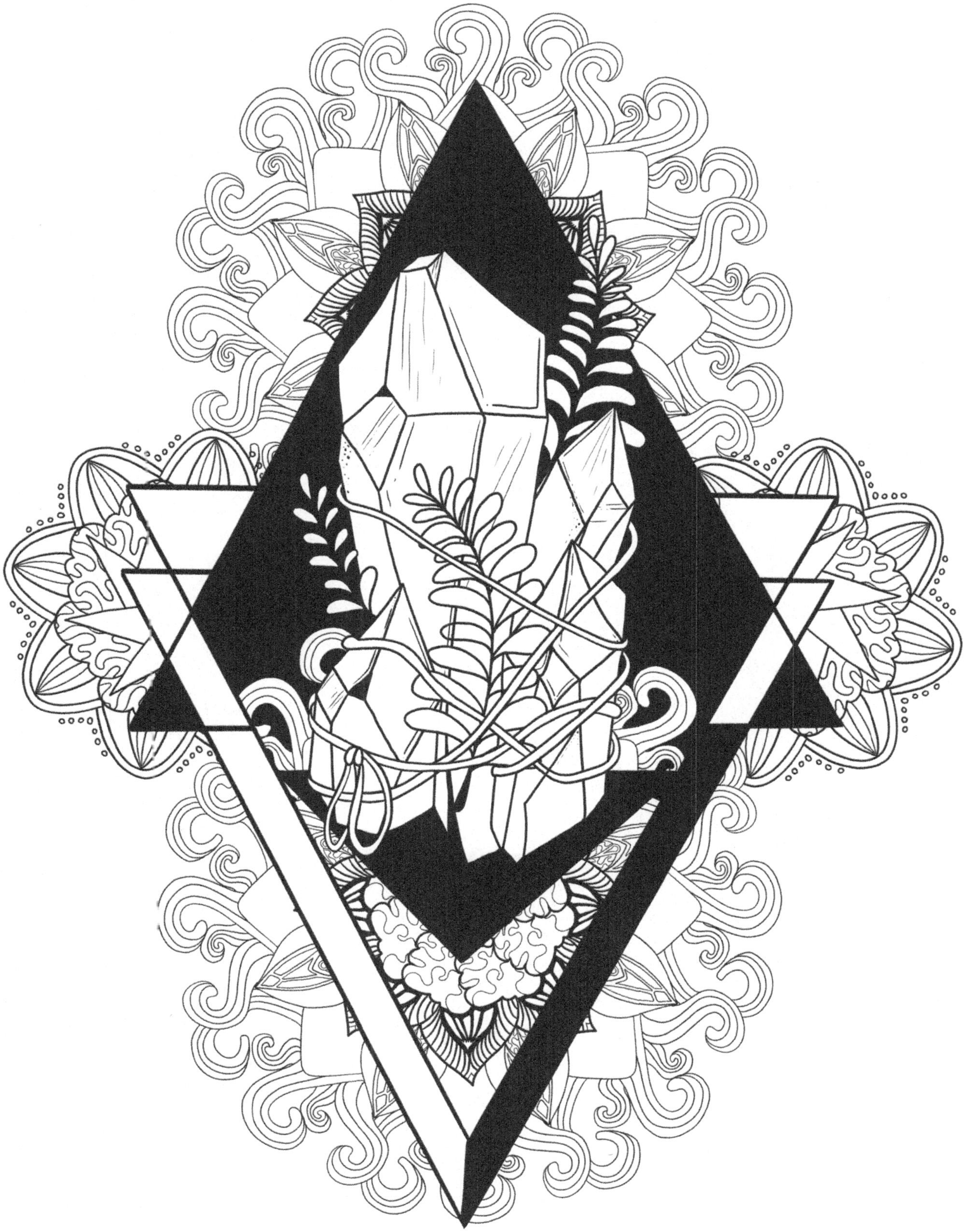

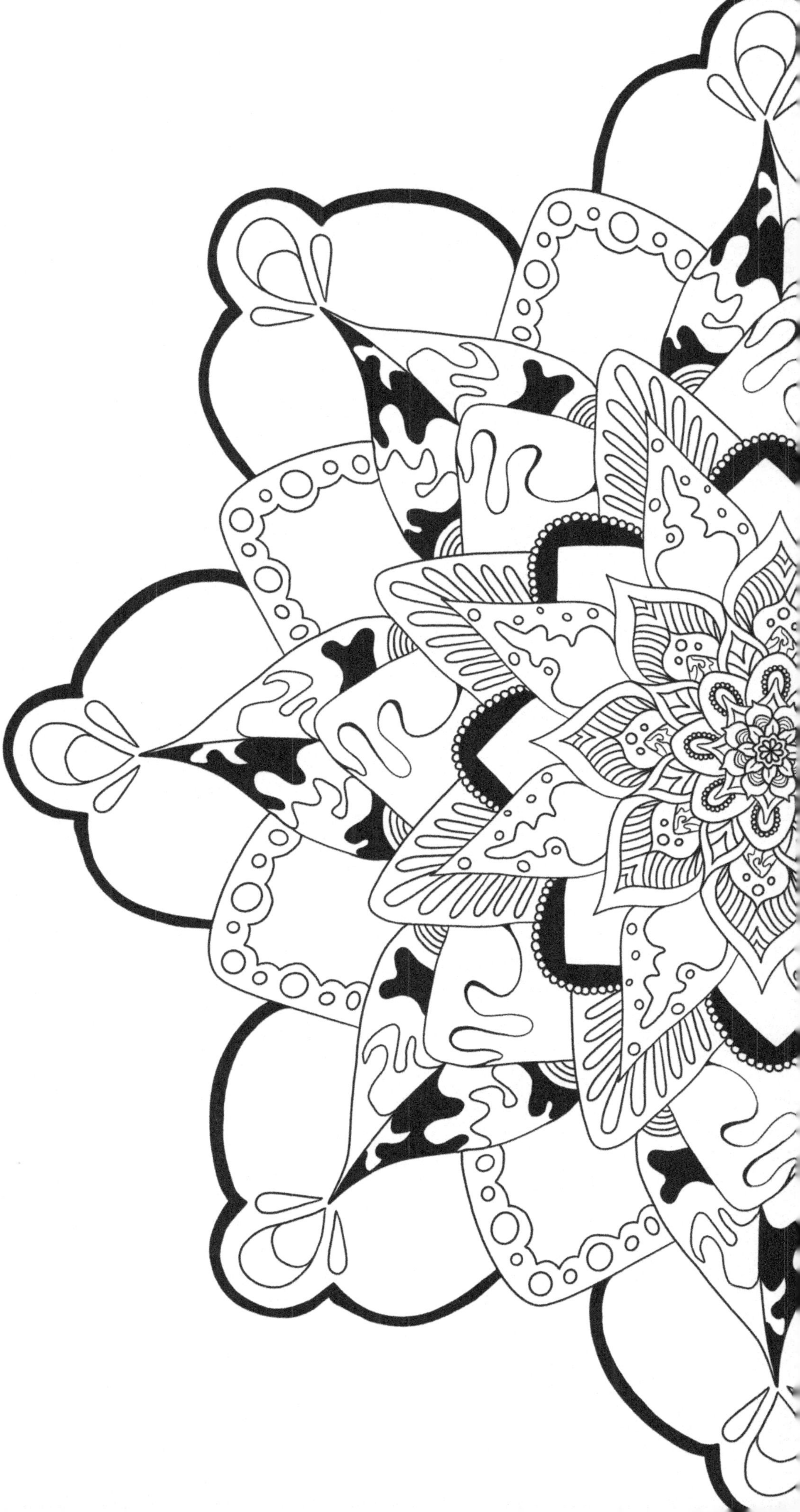

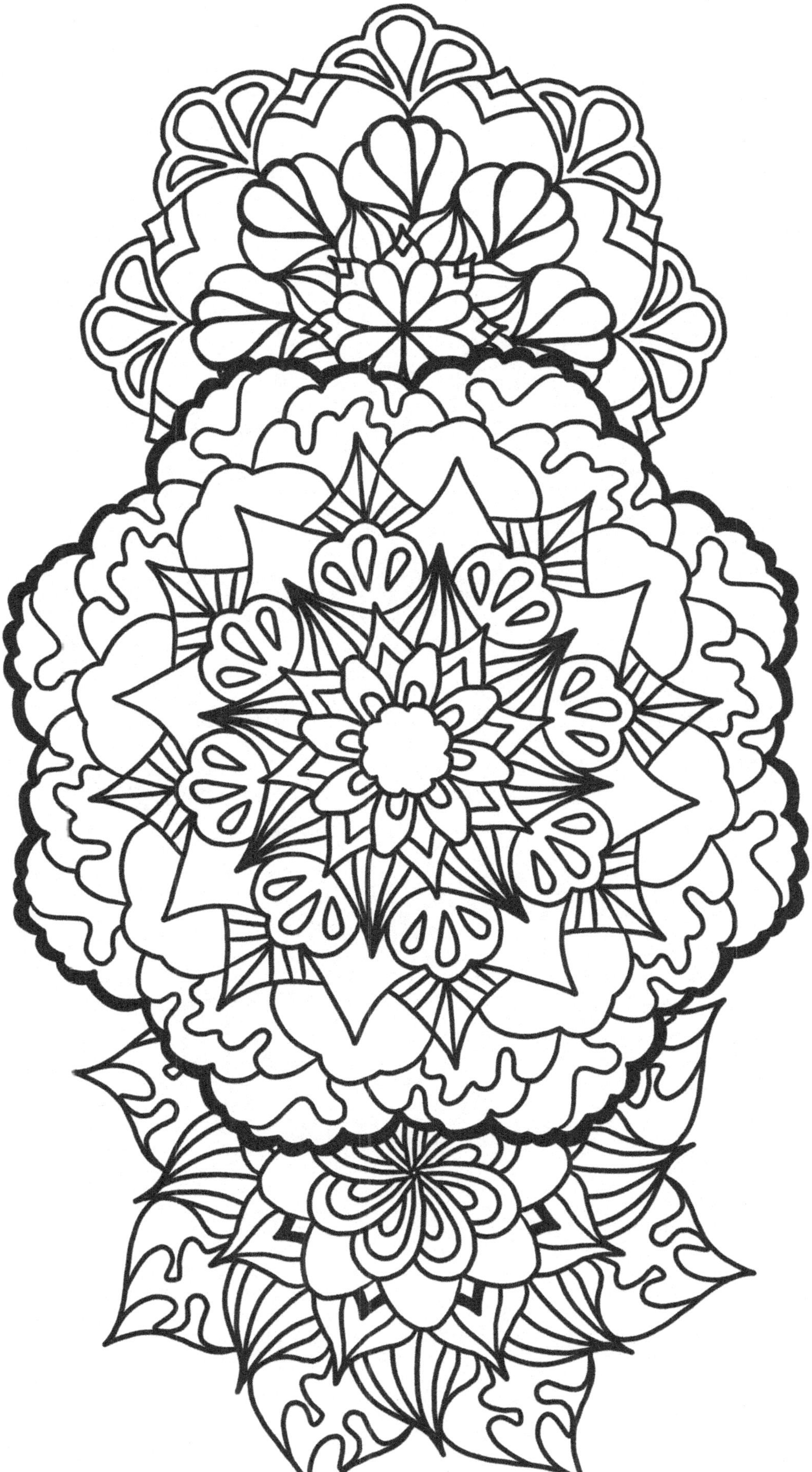

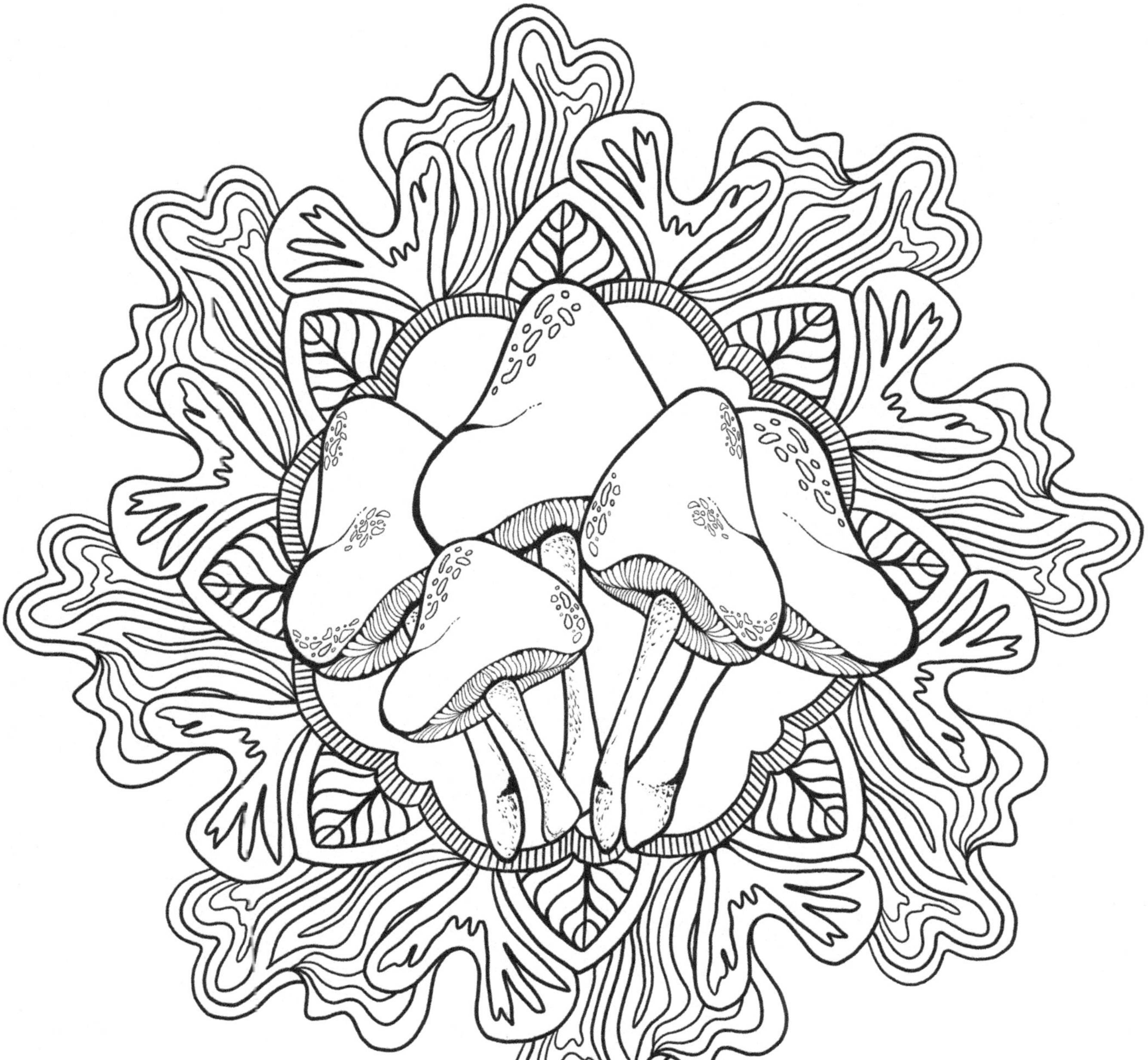

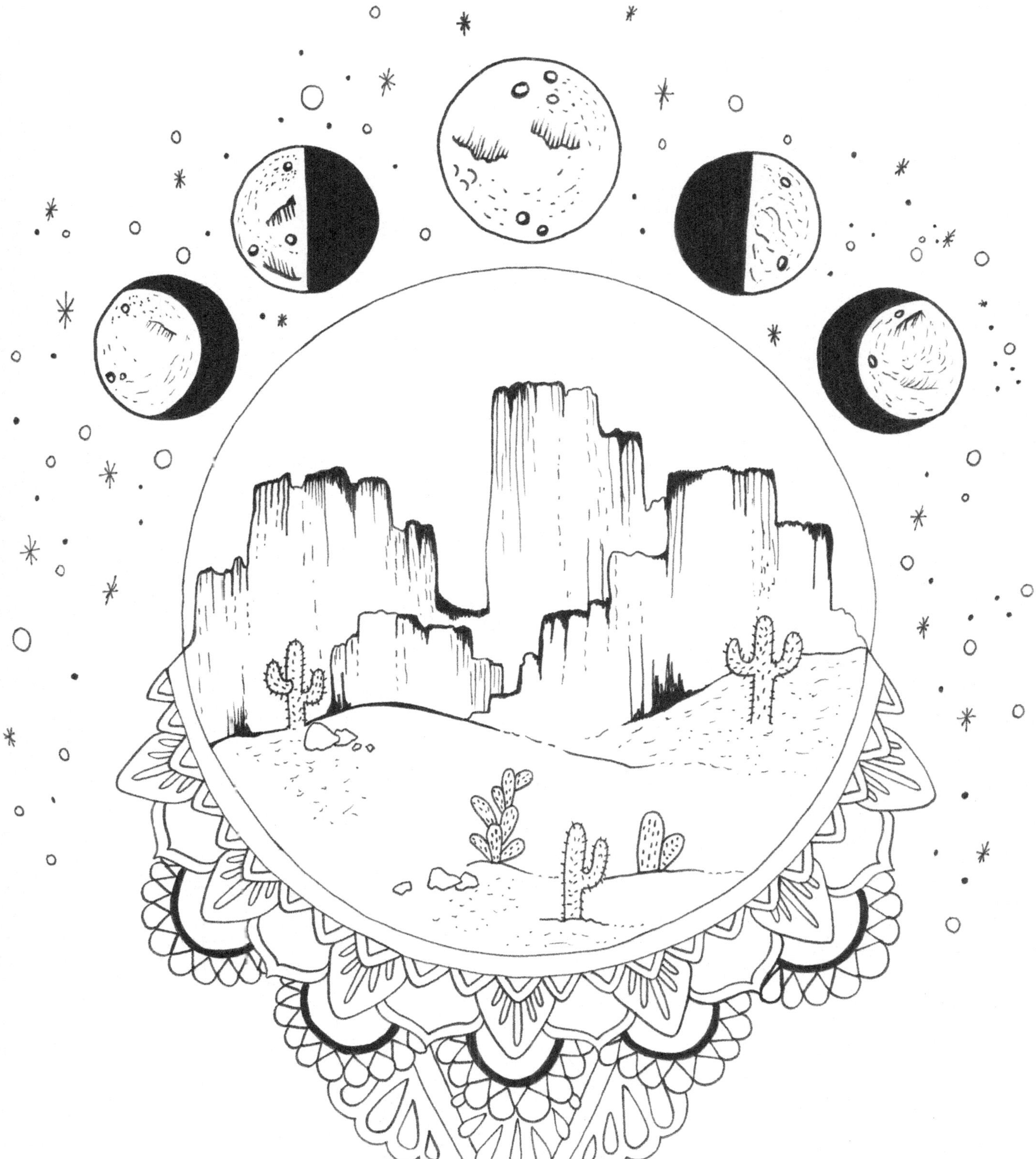

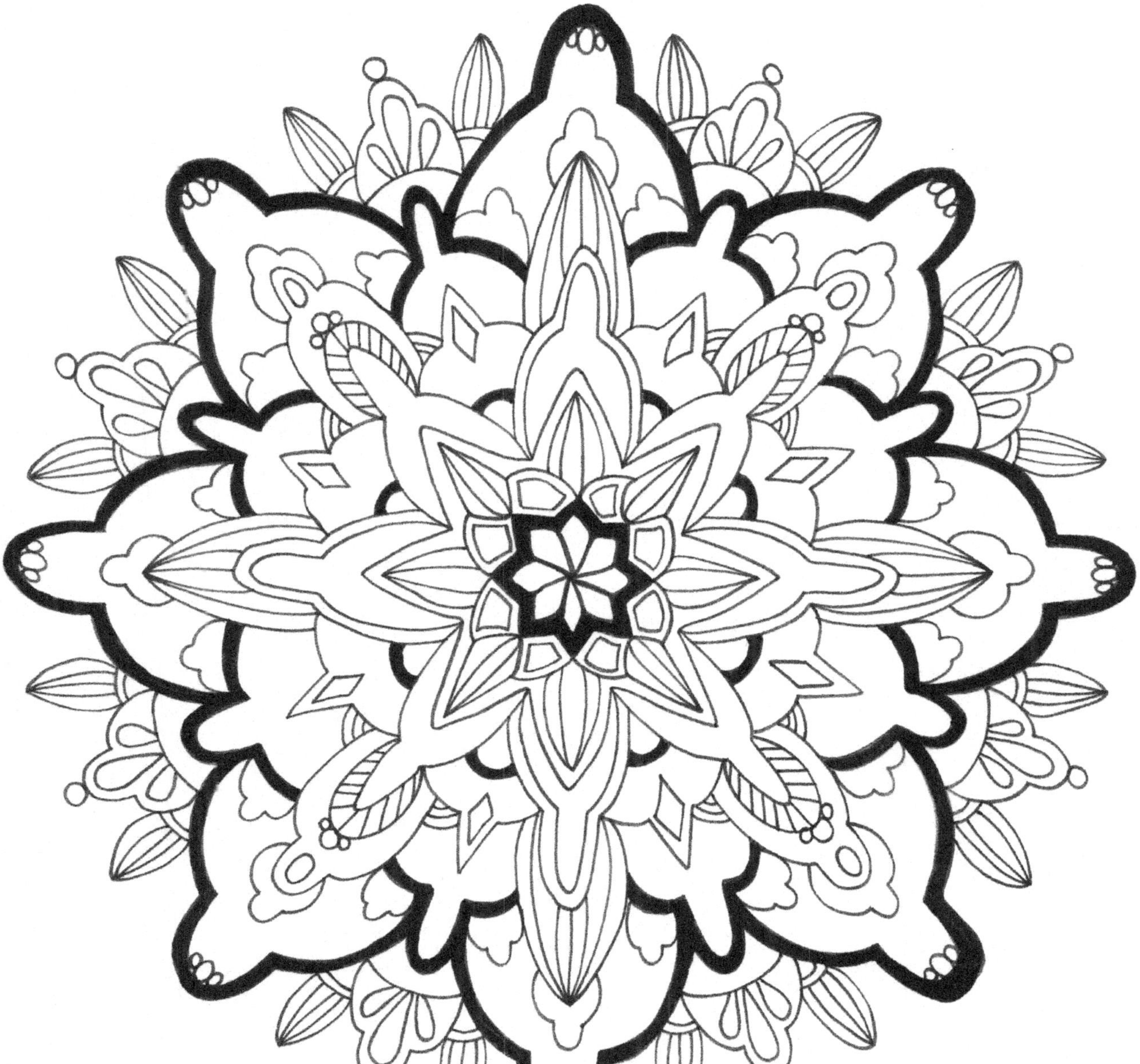

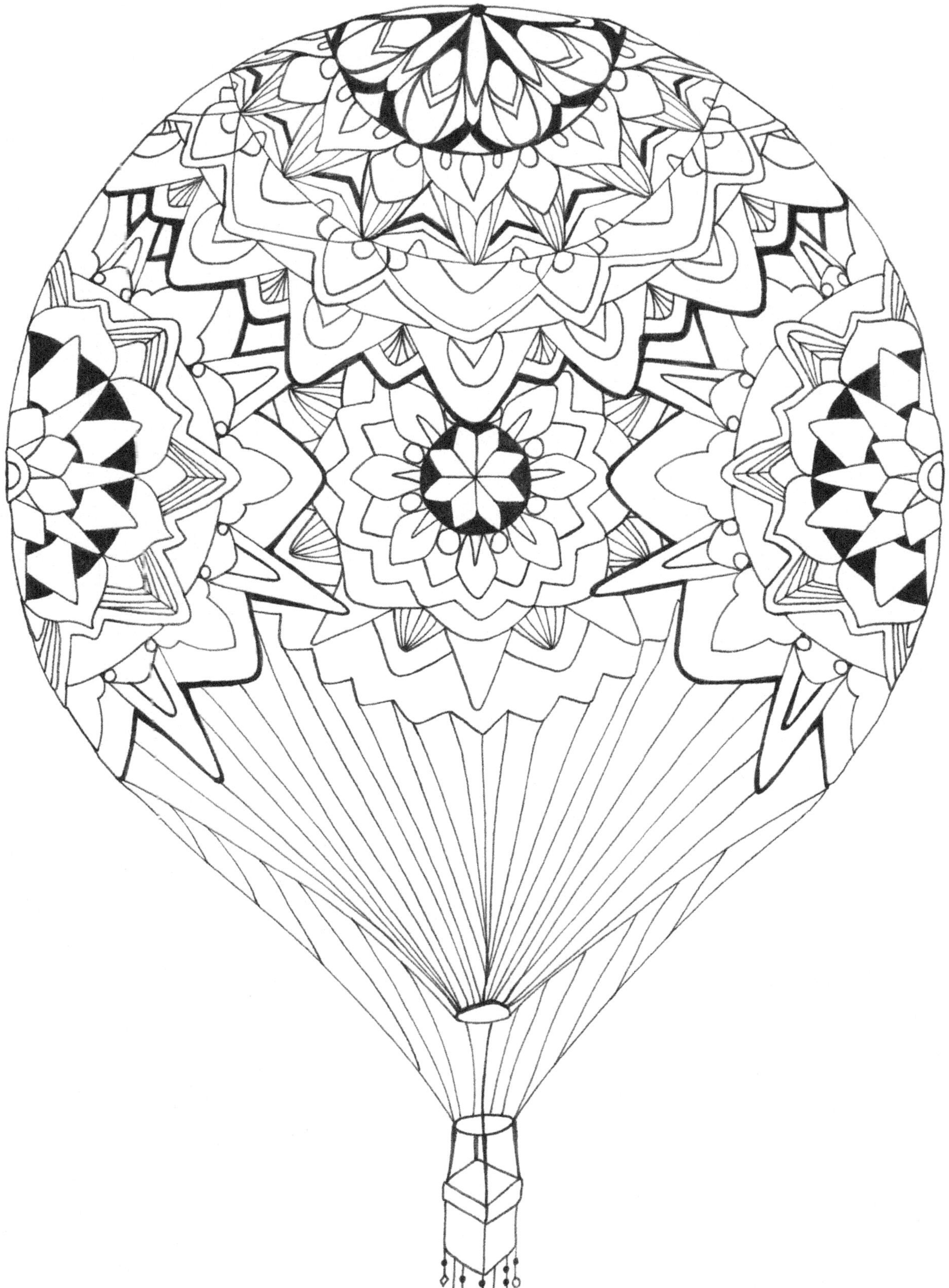

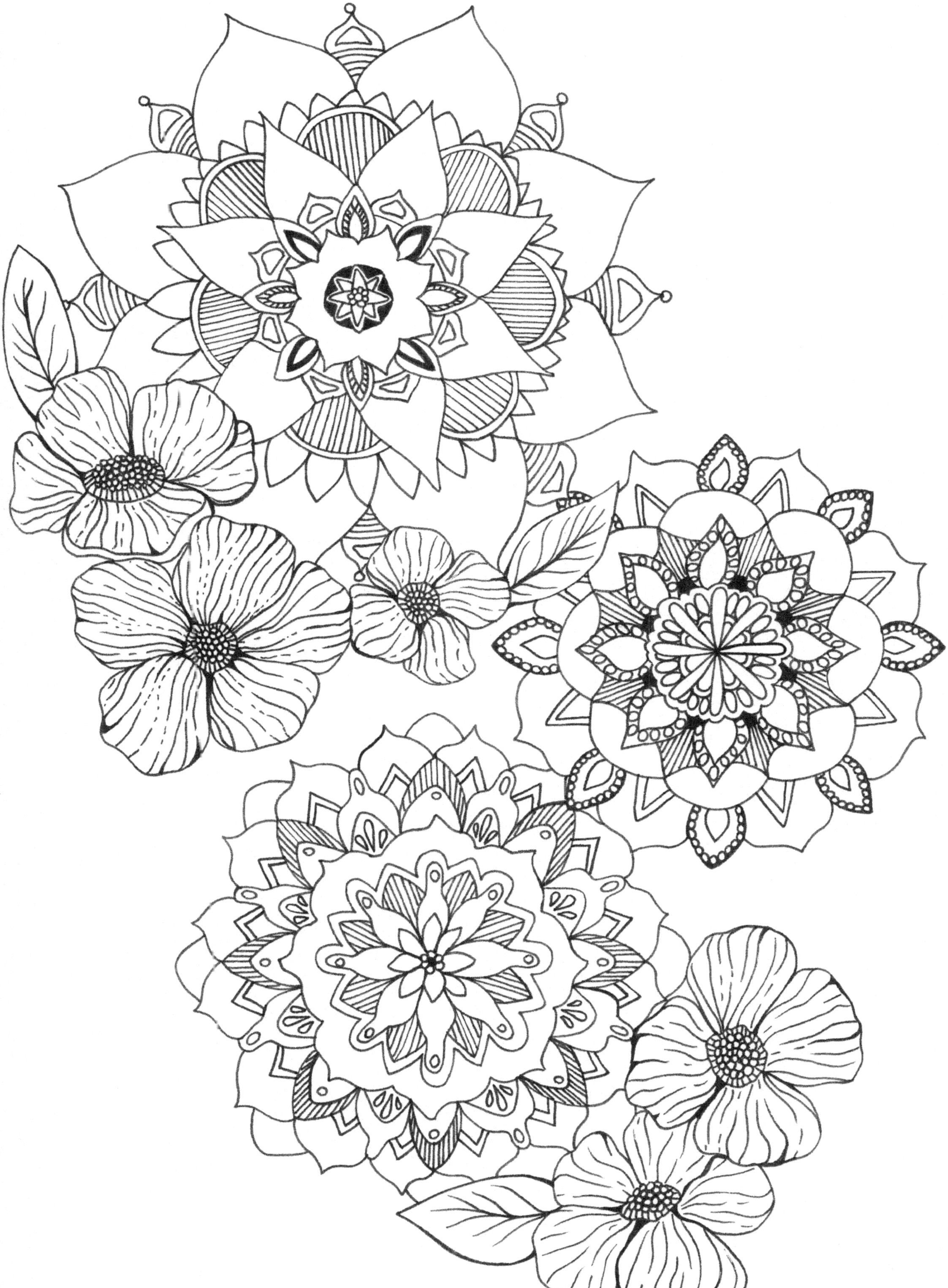

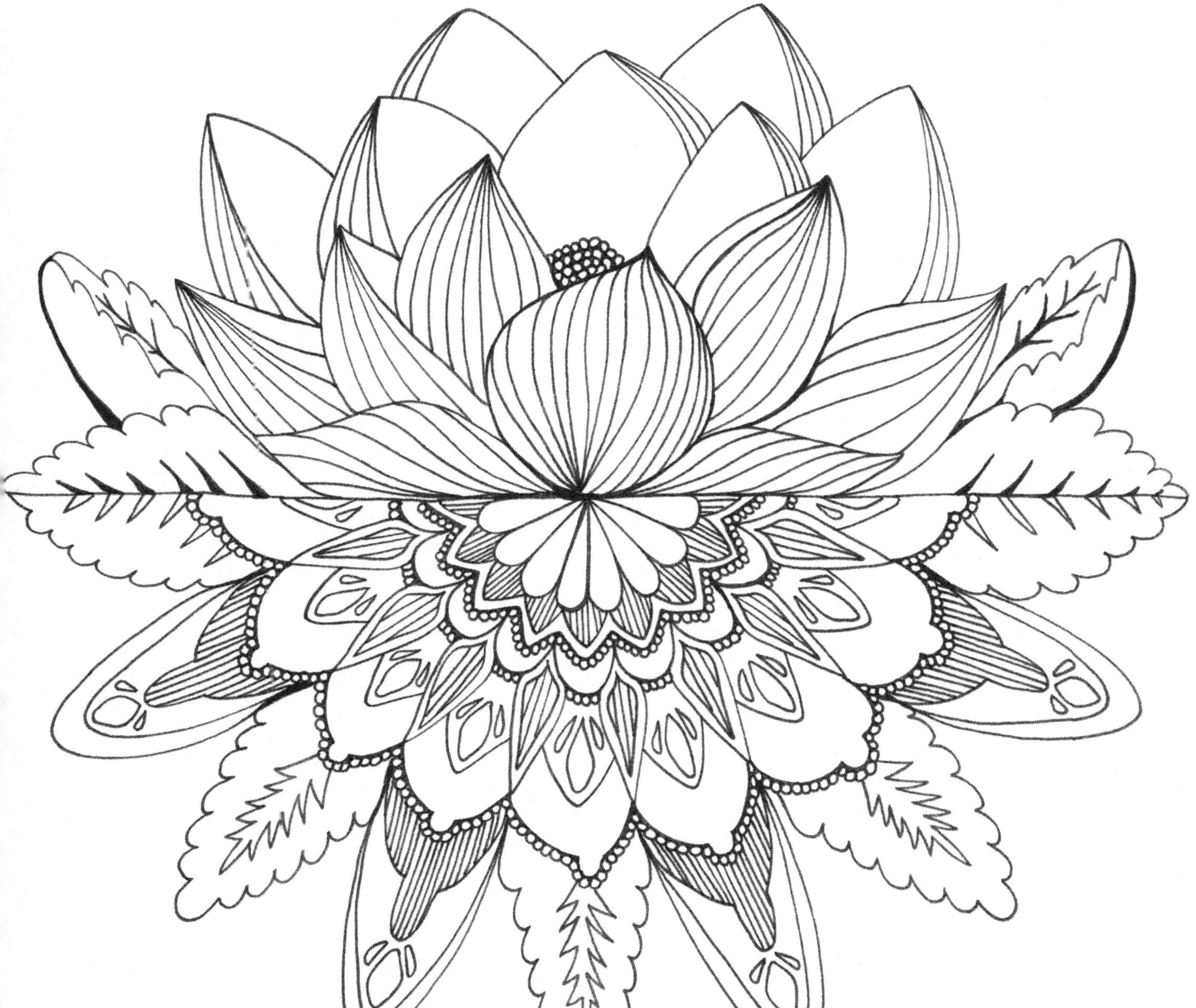

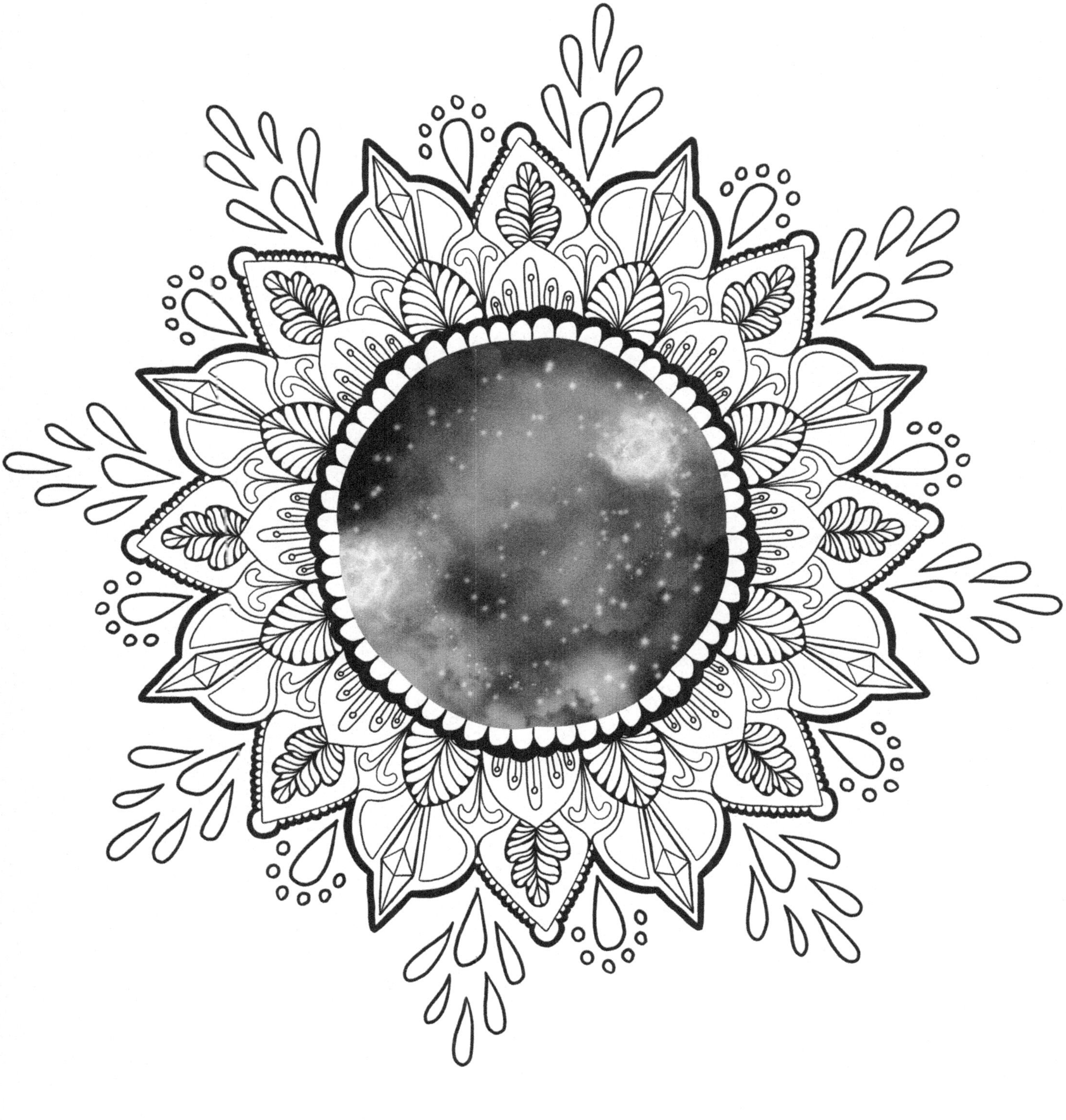

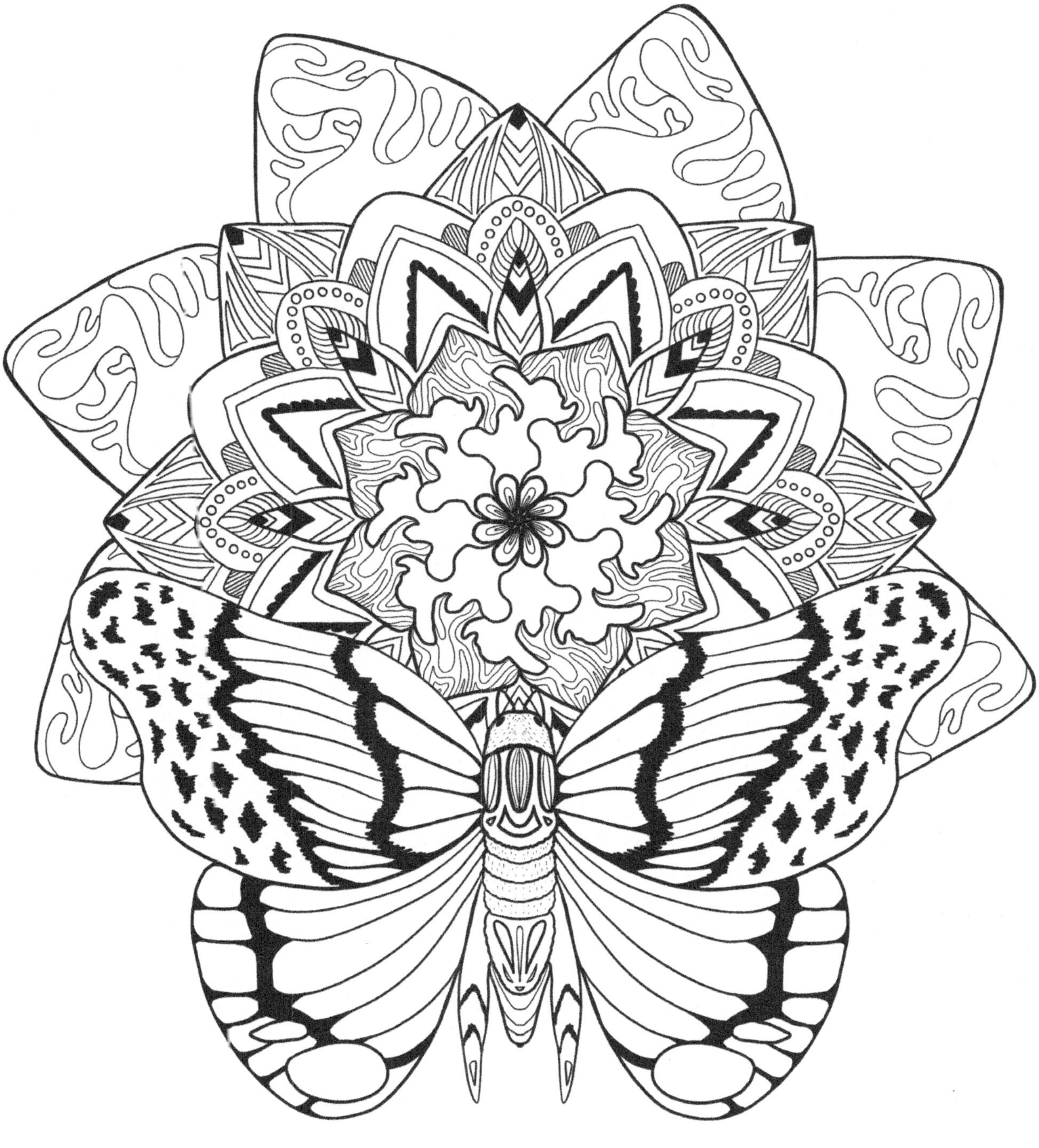

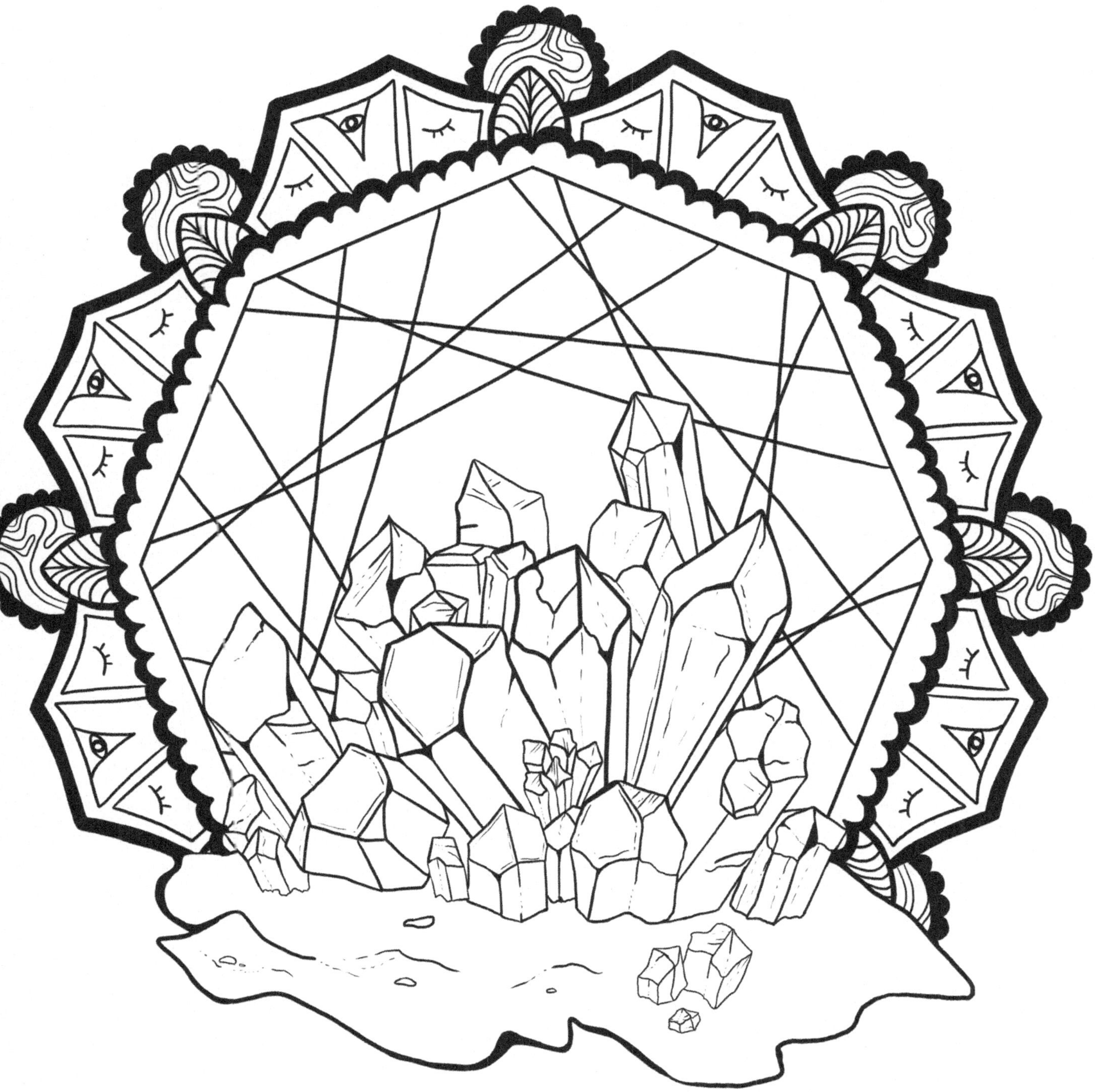

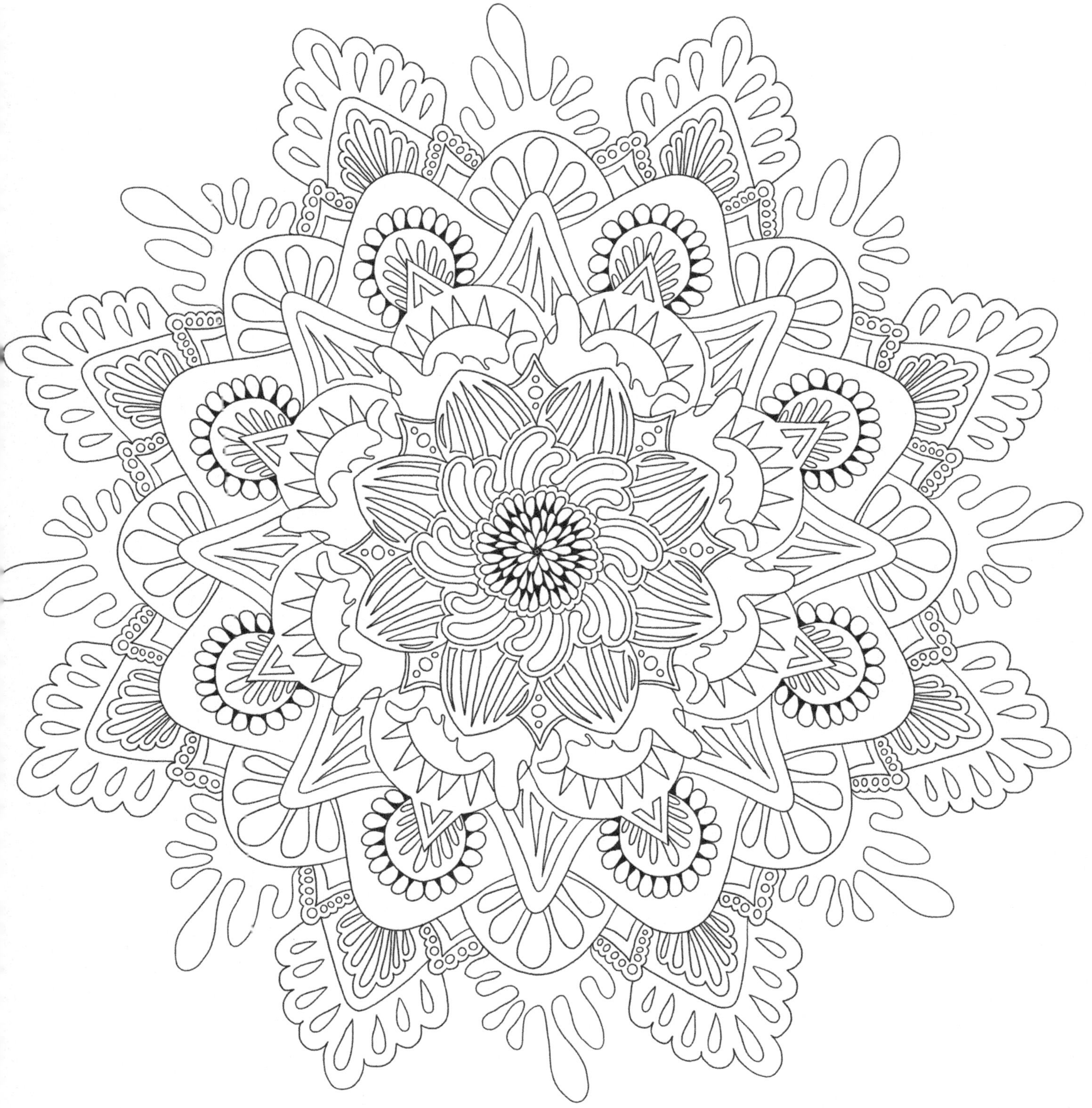

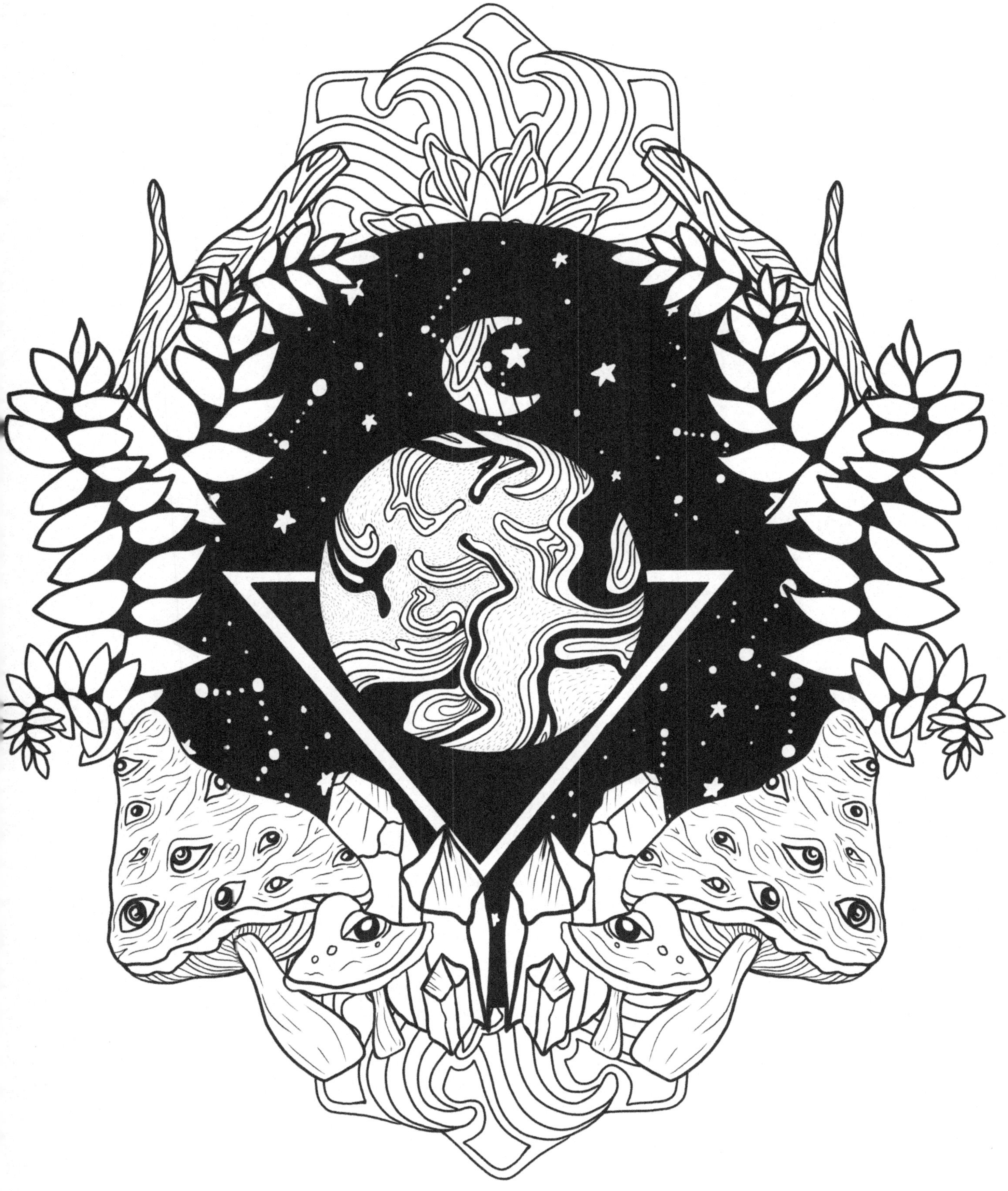

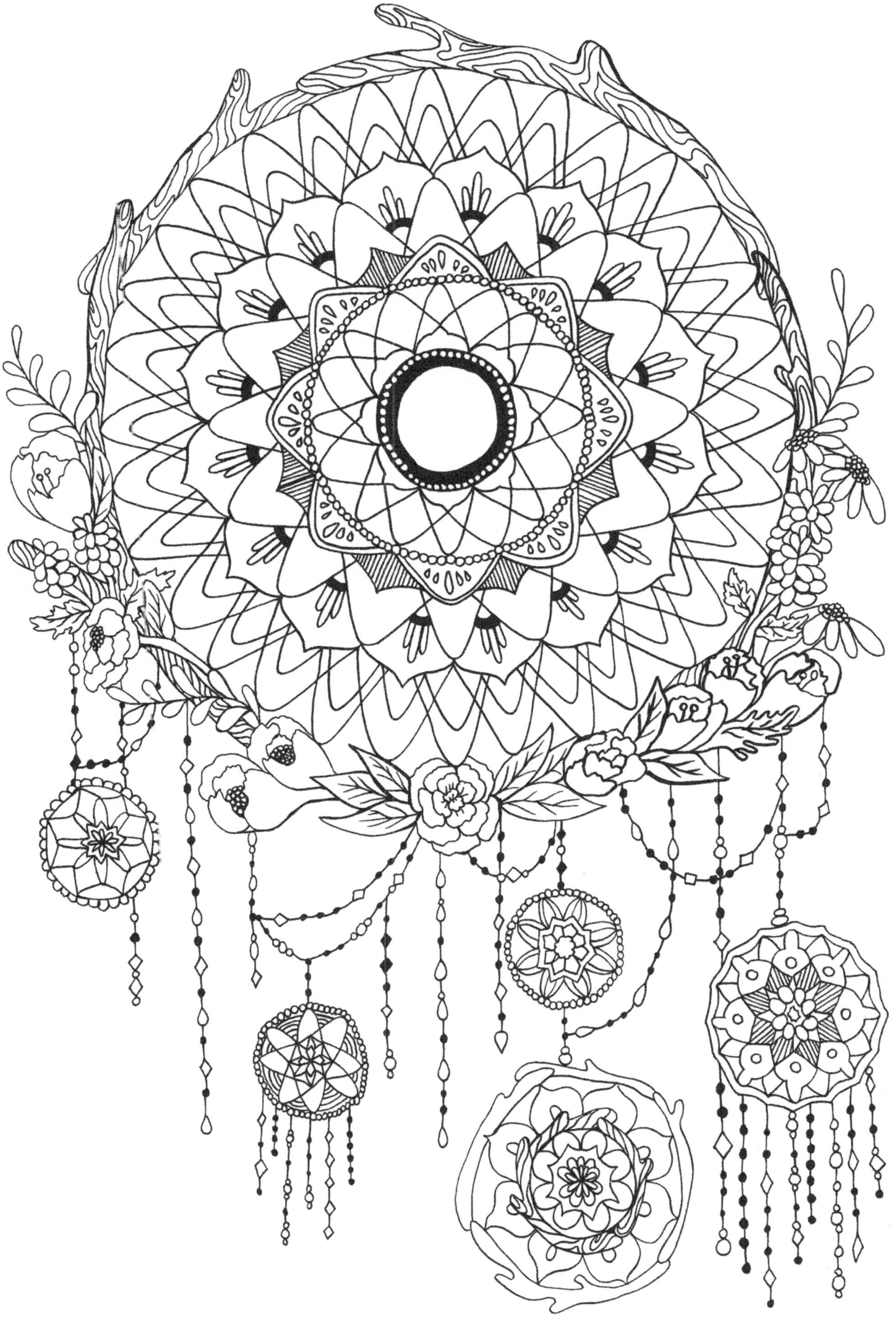

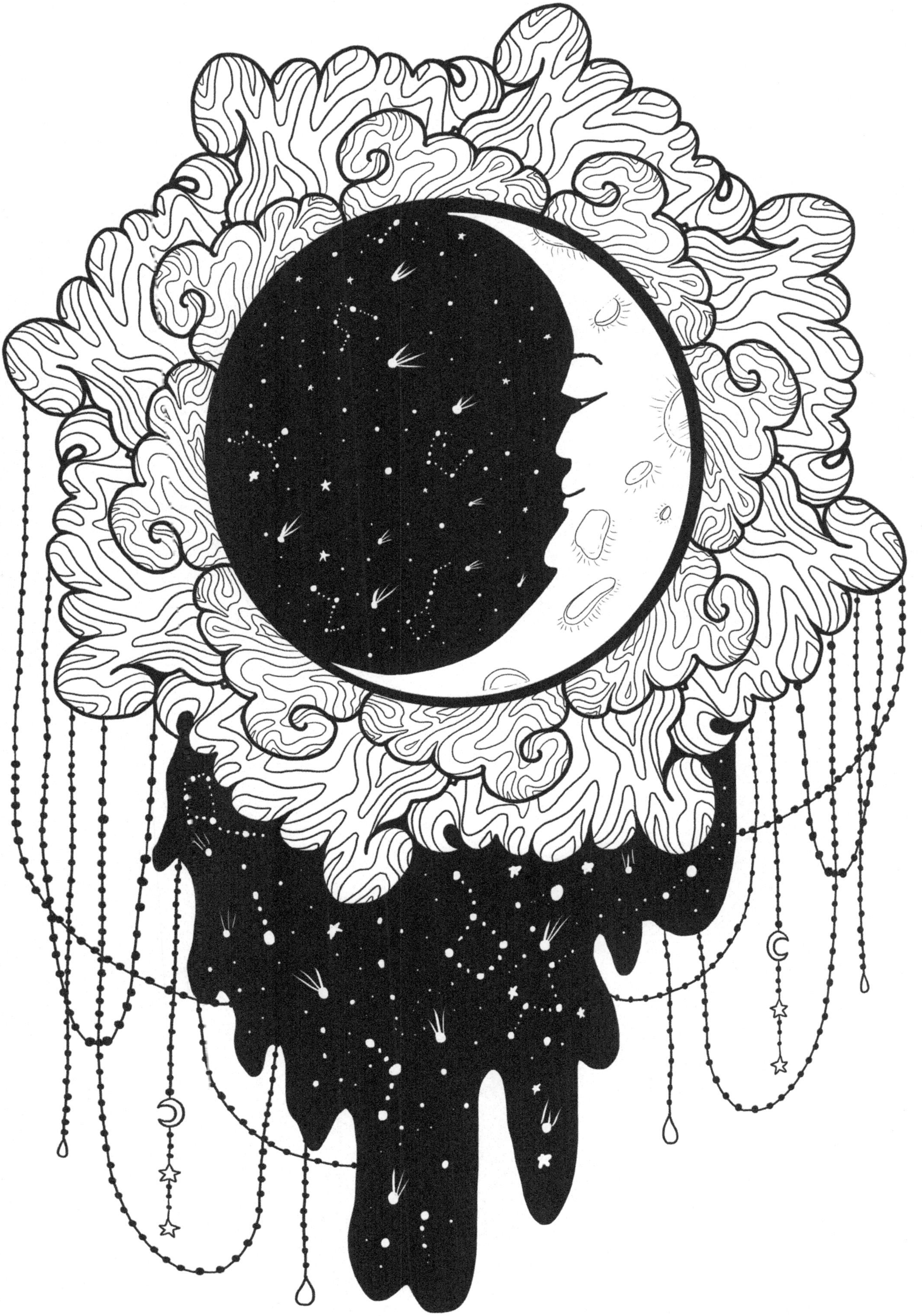

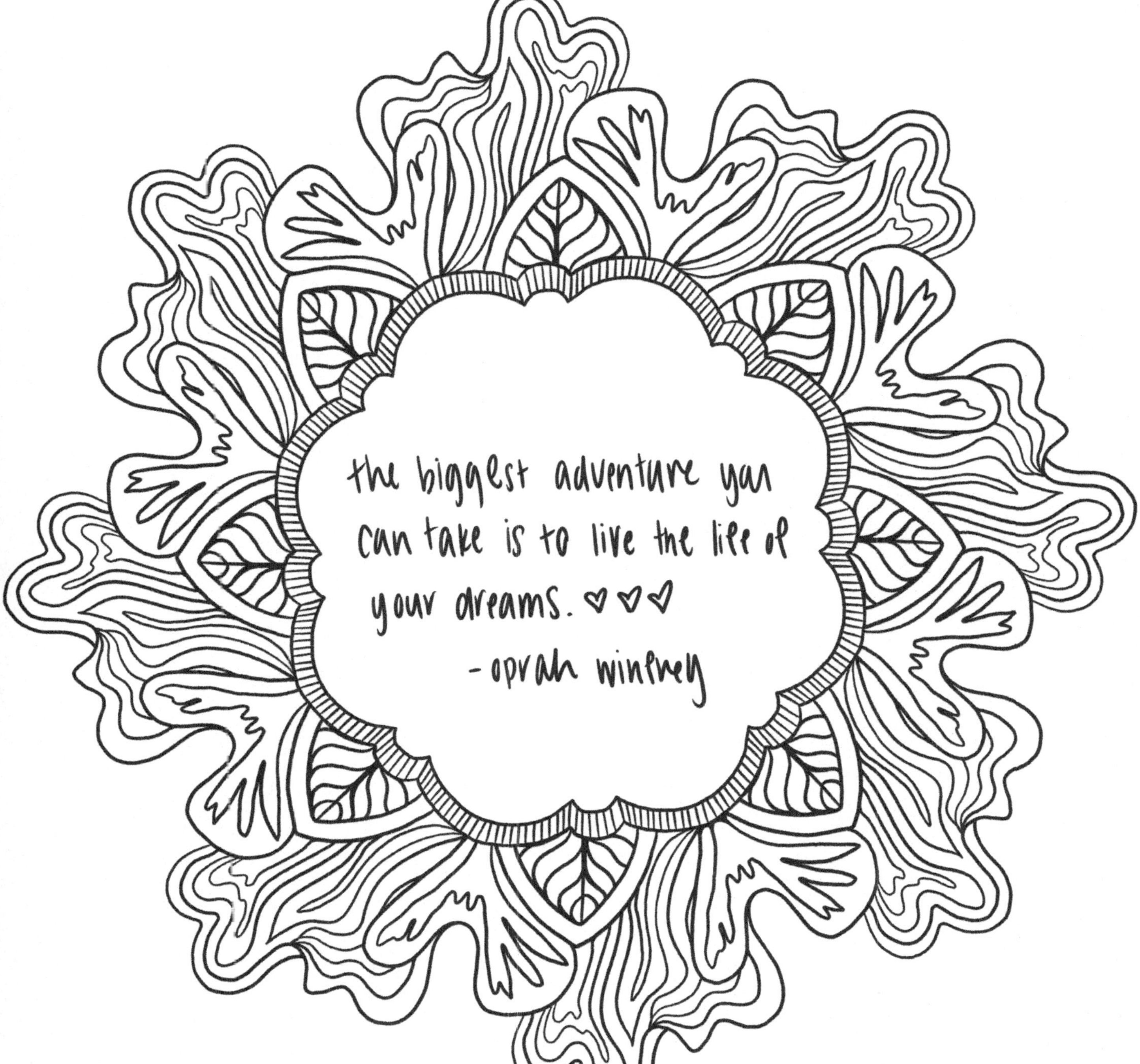

Thank you for your support. You make it possible for me to pursue my dream as an artist. If you enjoyed this book, please leave a review on Amazon!

Made in the USA
Middletown, DE
29 January 2020

83870689R00046